COMING HOME

THE SOUTHERN VERNACULAR HOUSE

James Lowell Strickland with *Terry Pylant*, *Todd Strickland*,
Aaron Daily, *Andrew Cogar*, and *Kevin Clark*
of HISTORICAL CONCEPTS

Written with *Susan Sully*

Editorial assistance by *Dawn M. Fritz*

Principal photography by *Richard Leo Johnson*

RIZZOLI
NEW YORK

New York · Paris · London · Milan

*To my family, with thanks for
your endless encouragement.*

*To the talented architects and
planners who have defined
the Old South—with gratitude
for your inspiration.*

— JAMES LOWELL STRICKLAND
HISTORICAL CONCEPTS

PAGE 1: *French doors surrounded by sidelights and transoms connect the interior of this Southern vernacular cottage with the lush landscape around it.* PAGE 2: *Soft blue shutters and crisp white decorative detailing bring renewed elegance to an updated 1920s cottage on Jupiter Island.* PAGES 4–5: *Drawing from vernacular agrarian traditions, a working cane mill and lakeside hunting lodge give this South Carolina property a picturesque beauty.* LEFT: *A collection of cherished family photographs hanging against simple tongue-and-groove walls adds a layer of generational history to this cozy sunroom.* PAGE 9: *With Greek Revival details, including square columns and a Classical entablature, this Lowcountry center-hall cottage is simultaneously formal and welcoming.*

CONTENTS

PREFACE

Historical Concepts was founded by Jim Strickland in 1982, several years after the Georgia native graduated from Yale University with a master's degree in architecture. At a time when few houses were being built in traditional styles, Strickland and his firm helped shape the future of Southern architecture by looking to the past for inspiration. Influenced by the region's great historic houses and their unnamed builders, as well as the South's most revered Classical Revival architects—Neel Reid, Philip Shutze, Edward Vason Jones, Lewis Crook, and James Means—Historical Concepts celebrates the warmth and charm that lies at the heart of Southern architecture.

For nearly thirty years, Strickland and his partners have designed residences in classical and Southern vernacular styles. Rather than conforming to strict canons of specific styles or periods, Historical Concepts creates homes that combine elements of traditional design with modern ways of living. Inspired by regional vernacular styles and the characteristics of the setting, whether rural or urban, these houses pay homage to and perpetuate the South's deep sense of place.

Since its inception, Historical Concepts has also provided "place-making" services that include land planning, design guidelines, and the creation of community and commercial buildings that complement their residential architecture. Communities in which the firm has participated include Spring Island, Palmetto Bluff, and Oldfield in South Carolina; River Dunes and Balsam Mountain Preserve in North Carolina; Celebration and WaterColor in Florida; and Sweet Bottom Plantation and The Ford Plantation in Georgia. Integrating lessons from the South's historic towns and neighborhoods, Strickland and his partners have developed homes, buildings, and streetscapes with authentic character and timeless appeal.

CLOCKWISE FROM UPPER LEFT: *In classic Southern style, sidelights and a transom surround this front door. A hayloft-style window and cupola draw from agrarian forms. This freestanding staircase in the Captain's House in River Dunes, North Carolina, makes a dramatic statement. The architecture and plan of River Dunes, located on the Pamlico Sound, is inspired by historic coastal towns in North Carolina and Virginia. Lattice and trelliswork add gardenesque elements to the Classical portico of this Shingle-style home. Chinoiserie at the Jupiter Island Club inspired the ornamental details on the entry of this early twentieth-century Colonial Revival house. A Chinese Chippendale railing and decorative arbor add whimsy to this tropical estate.*

Historical Concepts has received multiple awards for its residential and commercial architecture. In 2010, the firm's body of work was recognized with the Arthur Ross Award, the Institute of Classical Architecture & Art's highest accolade. The firm's work has also been featured extensively in publications devoted to architecture, interior design, and the building arts. This widespread recognition confirms Historical Concepts' philosophy of drawing from the past to design the architecture of today—and tomorrow.

With first-floor rooms arranged around a center hall and bedrooms tucked into steep gables, the central portion of this house is reminiscent of a Southern vernacular Carpenter Gothic cottage. Creating the impression that the house grew over time, asymmetrical wings with a series of screened and open-air porches extend on either side of the central mass.

COMING HOME

The notion of home is a strong one that evokes a personal anthology of memories. Whether it recalls the places where we lived as children, the houses of beloved grandparents where generations of family gathered together on special occasions, or even our secret dreams of home, the notion almost always conjures the sense of comfort, ease, and security that we all long for and strive to re-create.

For many Southerners, the words "coming home" instantly evoke the image of a porch where family and friends sip iced tea and share news—usually of the local kind. Or perhaps a veranda where they sit alone with half-closed eyes in a rocking chair, engulfed by jasmine-scented breezes. The setting might be the piazza of a single house in Charleston, a farmhouse porch with square posts and exposed rafters, or a rickety screened porch on an old beach house. The style and stature of the porch isn't what matters. What's important is the shelter provided beneath its overhang—familiar, inviting, and protective.

Jim Strickland has long thought about porches and the houses they grace. His fascination with Southern architecture got an early start as he grew up in Atlanta in the 1950s, traveling past the Classical Revival houses of Buckhead and West Paces Ferry Road on his way to school. Admiring the ease and elegance with which they addressed their surroundings, he was equally captivated by the humble country houses he drove by while accompanying his father on business calls to merchants in outlying counties. As the modest, white-painted dwellings slipped past the car window, he felt the tug of their invitation to slow down and step into a simpler way of life.

Southern houses have exerted a strong pull on Strickland throughout his career of designing residences that say "Welcome home" in this same old-fashioned way. Nowadays it's much easier for him to get inside the old homes that capture his eye and find out firsthand exactly how they weave their spell of welcome. The irregular width of old floorboards, the weight of solid brass hardware, the craftsmanship of the details—these are among the things he notices, whether in a rural cottage or a refined Neoclassical house.

The porch of this stately raised cottage overlooks the surrounding landscape through massive fluted columns. On either side of the deep porch, double-sash windows with overhead pockets open to a library and kitchen, maximizing light, ventilation, and views.

The architecture of the South is a rich and romantic vein from which to draw inspiration. Plantation houses rise like phantom temples from abandoned fields or stand in ruins tangled with kudzu vine. In small towns, merchants' homes with Greek Revival porches or Victorian towers fan out from drowsy main streets lined with rows of brick stores and county courthouses. Reminders of days when families lived more closely to the land, farms with tin-roofed houses and faded red barns spark nostalgia for less complicated times. In the region's most historic cities, pristinely restored mansions with freshly painted columns and re-pointed bricks recall the South's golden age of global commerce and sophistication.

LEFT: *Reminiscent of a West Indian plantation house, the façade of this Lowcountry dwelling features a series of French doors with solid shutters that open into a spacious central living area.* BELOW: *In this folly-like guesthouse, delicate latticework columns contrast playfully with the formality of the temple-style entablature and pediment.*

LEFT: *Painted plank walls with simple moldings create the perfect backdrop for a bobbin-leg table and sepia-tone painting of quail. Custom-made to fit this niche, they complement this farmhouse-style dwelling's rural yet refined character.* ABOVE: *Based on the design of an 1860s smokehouse, this guesthouse is embellished with a standing-seam copper roof and barn doors that slide open to reveal French doors leading to the great room within.*

The Neoclassical architecture of these cities speaks a unified language based on the architectural canons of ancient Greece and Rome. Spanning two centuries of style, residences in Georgian, Federal, and Greek Revival styles decorate the streets with columns crowned by Doric, Ionic, and Corinthian capitals. Within this Classical unity, however, vernacular variety reigns. In Savannah, the doors beneath most Federal porticos open into stair halls of attached, masonry town houses. In Beaufort, they lead into the center halls of freestanding dwellings with wide, white-clapboard façades, while in downtown Charleston, they swing into the shady side porches of single houses overlooking gardens planted with camellias and gardenias.

Outside urban centers, the vernacular styles and forms range even more widely. From primitive dogtrot houses with ground-floor rooms flanking open-air passageways to four-square farmhouses with wraparound porches, they have one thing in common: providing comfort in a hot climate. Designed with function in mind, they demonstrate creative solutions to living at ease with their surroundings. While these solutions are practical—plentiful windows for cross ventilation, metal roofs that deflect the sun's rays, and shutters that control its light—they also provide pleasures nearly forgotten in the modern world. Morning breezes blowing across a bedroom, rain on a tin roof, and stripes of shade cast by louvered shutters address the senses, connecting those who live in such houses with the here and now.

The houses of the rural South also forge a strong connection with the natural world. In isolated mountain regions where rock and timber were the only available building materials, log houses set on stone foundations are virtually indistinguishable from their woodland setting. Early coastal houses with foundations of handmade brick or tabby—a concrete made from crushed oyster shells—rise quite literally from the ground on which they stand. Just one step removed from their natural state, the rough-hewn beams and hand planed planks of such houses endow them with an essential beauty that requires no formal decoration.

There is something deeply reassuring about living in houses where the materials bear the mark of human hands. Their subtle imperfections remind us of the people who built them and their intention to protect and nurture generations of inhabitants. In these ways, the vernacular houses of the South speak not just of places, but also of people. Filled with collective memories, they invite us to make our own. When we step inside, we are never alone. When we sit on their porches, we hear the voices and laughter of those who came before us and know that we are home.

— SUSAN SULLY

Inspired by farm buildings with central passageways for wagons and carriages, this building at The Ford Planta-tion in Georgia functions as both living quarters and garage. In addition to parking, the lower level houses a potting shed and mudroom. Loft-like quarters above include a living room lit by a cupola, a bedroom, office, and small kitchen.

20

LEFT: *In this Ford Plantation carriage house, the bedroom has pine plank ceilings and floors of oak reclaimed from an old post office.* ABOVE: *Intended to resemble a closed-in porch, this charming potting shed is outfitted with simple cabinets with vintage-style hardware.*

INSPIRATION

---

*You cannot impart
the warmth and wisdom
that comes with age
without understanding
that which came before.*

STANDING BEFORE the fine eighteenth- and nineteenth-century houses of the South and their humble vernacular counterparts, it's impossible not to admire the thought and love that went into their design and construction. Having evolved in response to specific conditions—climate, cultural traditions, and regional ways of life—they tell us so much about our ancestors and the lives they led.

The preservation of historical architecture is essential to keeping these lessons alive. The rescue of Savannah's Davenport House in 1955 by the ladies who founded the Historic Savannah Foundation is a vital source of inspiration. After touring the house for the first time, I became aware of the necessity of perpetuating traditional design and historical precedent in modern-day architectural practice. This trip to Savannah led to travels in other historic places to document individual houses and explore the communities, towns, and cities they comprise. An essential part of the way I work, urban and architectural pilgrimages are now regular practice for the firm.

Savannah and the other great cities of the South, including Charleston, Annapolis, Baltimore, and New Orleans, are all touchstones for us. Each has a distinct architectural character and streetscape, from the orderly grids of Savannah and New Orleans' French Quarter to the meandering streets and lanes south of Broad Street in Charleston. While the stately, iconic houses that line these cities' avenues and squares are impressive, the narrow alleyways and humble outbuildings behind them are just as fascinating. On any given tour of Southern cities, we spend as much time looking at the backs of buildings as their fronts.

Architectural expeditions also lead us to small Southern cities and towns such as Columbus and Macon, Georgia, and Beaufort and Rockville, South Carolina. In these, we discover the widely varying vernacular expressions of Classical styles. When a native Beaufortonian took us on a tour of the city's homes, for instance, we noticed a regional variation of the classic Federal house plan that had evolved to enhance cross ventilation in a sultry climate. With wraparound porches designed to capture waterborne breezes, the formal houses assumed an easy charm ideal for coastal living, inspiring us to design new houses that combine their grace and comfort.

Equally intriguing are the buildings that lie outside cities and towns, down country roads, or in small coastal and mountain communities where Southerners have summered for

PAGE 25: *The entrance of the William Gibbes House, one of Charleston, South Carolina's, finest Adamesque residences, offers iconic examples of the period's style, including an engaged portico in the mutulary Doric order and ornate geometric patterns at the sidelights and transom.* LEFT: *The design and execution of this window in Charleston illustrates the love of fine woodworking brought to America from England. The fit of the shutter and handiwork of the strap hinges exemplify the artistry and craftsmanship of the past.*

generations. These buildings reveal the unrefined handiwork of country carpenters working with rudimentary tools and readily available materials. In early twentieth-century cottages, the unpretentious charm of tin roofs, beadboard walls, and quirky rooms carved out from porches invites anyone who enters to slow down and relax. In old farmhouses, barns, or mountain cabins, the fragrance of cypress beams and pine planks creates an instant, visceral connection with the past. As demolition and the passage of time take their toll, memories of these humble structures are in danger of fading away.

The form, craftsmanship, and materials of individual buildings are important, but we never look at these without also considering context—how do they fit within their natural surroundings or form part of a neighborhood or an urban setting? In historic cities and small towns, the shifts in size, style, and materials among the main street buildings provide character and an intimate experience of discovery. Not every building makes a statement, and this contributes to an atmosphere where excitement is balanced by calm. By practicing these principles in neo-traditional communities like Palmetto Bluff, South Carolina, and River Dunes, North Carolina, we can design streetscapes with authentic small-town character.

Although deeply engaged with the built environment of the South, we never lose sight of the architecture of the Northeast, in part because of its historic influence down the Eastern Seaboard. For a mountaintop retreat in the Blue Ridge Mountains, the Great Camps of the Adirondacks informed the look of camp-style cottages and a rustic dining hall. Many of the architectural details of a new house in Bridgehampton reflect discoveries we made during a tour of old towns in the Hamptons and of whalers' cottages in Nantucket.

Farther South, the idiosyncratic buildings and varied street plan of Coral Gables, near Miami, serve as a rich and wonderful prototype for New Urbanism. In Key West, we were intrigued by the architectural diversity, distinct vernacular styles, and pedestrian-friendly density, which were later expressed in designs for individual houses and residential developments.

Wherever we go, small details like the depth of a windowsill, the shape of a wrought-iron stair rail, or the vestiges of milk paint on a reclaimed pine plank capture our attention. Inspiration comes from the past and the present, the urban and the rural, the classical and indigenous, the intricate and simple. It is everywhere, if you have the eyes to see.

TOP: *The covered walkway of an old hotel in Eufaula, Alabama, now converted for commercial use, demonstrates the human scale and hand-constructed texture of Southern small-town streetscapes.* LOWER LEFT: *The weathered, uneven profile of this shutter and its hand-forged hardware speak of history and the passage of time.* LOWER RIGHT: *With a hand-crimped metal roof that slopes over a porch with simple railings, this country cottage conveys a sense of integrity.*

OPPOSITE PAGE, CLOCKWISE FROM TOP: *A Greek Revival outbuilding of a mansion outside Oxford, Mississippi, has inspired similar buildings in planned and traditional communities. In Savannah's Davenport House, traditional craftsmanship elevates a simple arched door surround into something of great beauty. Even unassuming commercial buildings in Savannah, Georgia, were constructed with care and detail.* LEFT: *A pierced railing adds character and charm to an 1830s house in Decatur, Georgia.* BELOW: *This five-bay house in Mobile, Alabama, reflects the changing scale of development in the late nineteenth and early twentieth centuries, when plantations began to be subdivided into smaller lots.*

SPIRIT OF STYLE

*There is a common language
that makes each style
recognizable, but the
idiosyncrasies that vary
from region to region and
house to house are what
define its spirit.*

THE QUESTION OF WHAT LEADS US to the style of a house is not easily answered. It may sound counterintuitive, but we rarely enter the design process with the idea of faithfully reproducing a specific style. Rather, the natural setting, the region's architecture, and the vision of the client are our guides. As a result, the style in which a house is built evolves gradually in a way that is never forced or unnatural.

The characteristics of the site always form our starting point because the vernacular styles that inspire us responded practically and creatively to their surroundings. If the setting is natural, the shape of the land, the density of the trees, or the lack thereof affect matters of style. In urban and suburban sites, the scale, form, decoration, and materials of the nearby houses play an equally important role. Whatever the setting, it's essential to pay attention to the climate, the direction from which the breeze blows, and where the sun sets, just as our forebears did.

From a broader perspective, style is determined by region. By walking along small-town sidewalks, touring houses in historic cities, and happening upon old farmhouses down country roads, we gain insights into local architectural traditions. Whether looking at fine Classical houses or rural dwellings, we don't simply identify the particular style or period in which they are built. We study the craftsmanship, the materials, and the details—the thickness of a particular windowsill or the beading around a certain door. Subtle idiosyncrasies like these express the nuance of style. By observing them, we learn to create houses with a deep feeling of authenticity and appropriateness to their surroundings.

A waterfront bluff in Spring Island, South Carolina, reminded us of nearby Beaufort. For the design of a home on this site, we drew directly from Beaufort's historic architecture, creating a dignified façade with the proportions and details of an eighteenth-century Federal house. Throughout the house, we also integrated less formal but equally authentic vernacular elements, including painted buttboard walls and an enclosed rear porch. From the exquisite craftsmanship of the front door's fanlight to the simple carpentry of the walls, the house draws from the region's traditions to create a refined dwelling that is also relaxed enough for modern living.

The South's rural farmhouses and coastal cottages offer just as many lessons about style as its Classical dwellings. Often utilitarian and unembellished, they have an unpretentious charm that embodies the practical values of people living in harmony with their surroundings.

Style is determined by so many elements—geography, history, climate—but personal aesthetics and ideas about home have always been among the most important. Houses should not just be academic exercises in proven architectural canons. They need to *feel* right, both in the places where they stand and to the people who live in them. The houses we design may seem familiar, but they are never facsimiles. Inspired by intuition and imagination, they are individual responses to place, time, and the visions of those who will inhabit them.

PAGE 33: *Large fluted columns reminiscent of the South's Greek Revival plantation houses rise two stories tall, supporting a portico that shades a gracious porch and second-story balcony.* ABOVE: *In contrast to a more formal center hall configuration, this lateral entry hall demonstrates a simplified approach to the Greek Revival style, which found expression in the South's smaller plantation houses. Interior shutters act as a screen, dividing the hall from the living area beyond, contributing an informal, vernacular element that is both functional and unexpected.*

The Road Home

RICEBORO, GEORGIA

The path that leads to the style of a house is often filled with surprising twists and turns. For this 1,200-acre tract of land bisected by the oldest road in Georgia, our client imagined a modest plantation house reminiscent of those near his hometown of Statesville, Georgia. In response, we proposed a simple raised dwelling in an understated vernacular style. During the design process, however, the discovery that flood elevations required the house to stand ten feet above the ground instead of five altered our plans significantly.

As we attempted to rework our original design with a higher foundation, it became clear that the proportions wouldn't work. The new elevation required a building of greater stature—a realization that sparked recollections of the Louisiana and Mississippi plantation houses of the Natchez Trace. Often Classical in style and raised above the ground to accommodate utilitarian spaces, these houses suggested a historical solution both to the higher elevation and statelier dimensions the site demanded.

To reconcile the larger scale of the new house with the unimposing appearance our client desired, we also looked to the mid-nineteenth-century raised cottages of New Orleans' Garden District. Ranging in style from the highly decorated to the restrained, they share carefully balanced proportions that keep them from dominating the street. Seen from the sidewalk, these houses appear approachable in scale—until someone comes out onto the porch and stands by the front door or a window. Only then do you realize how grand they really are.

Applying these lessons of scale and proportion, we designed a plantation-style dwelling that sits comfortably on our client's land and the river at its edge. Like many riverside plantations, the house has twin façades—one for those who approach by water, and one for travelers by land. In the Greek Revival style, the façades combine round columns and square pilasters to support a heavy entablature and broad, hipped roof. With simple Doric capitals instead

Flanked by fluted columns, the front door of this Greek Revival–style house opens into a central living hall. Doors surrounded by sidelights and a transom on either end of the hall lead to identical porches overlooking the land and the river. Heavy wood doors with solid brass hardware, period lighting, and antique furnishings contribute to the house's nineteenth-century appearance.

of Corinthian ones, the façades appear more inviting than monumental. Although they are large, the thick columns, wide entablature, and four-by-ten-foot windows play tricks with scale, visually reducing the building's size and tempering its grandeur.

Beneath the shade of the porches, tall doors swing into a symmetrical receiving hall that extends the full depth of the house. At both ends, double-hung windows tall enough to walk through invite cross ventilation and frame expansive views. Fireplaces with weighty Greek Revival mantels face each other across the room, warming two comfortable seating areas. From the heavy flared door surrounds to the eighteen-inch crown molding, all the architectural elements in the room are large in scale. Like those outside, they quiet the space and prevent its grand proportions from overwhelming.

In a typical center-hall plan, four rooms flank the receiving hall—a dining room and kitchen on the right and a library and master bedroom on the left. Slender pilasters and mural panels depicting Lowcountry landscapes give the dining room a gracious atmosphere befitting a Southern plantation.

Inspired by nineteenth-century Greek Revival plantations along the Natchez Trace, the façade combines square pilasters and round columns to create an effect that is both stately and graceful. On the waterfront side of the house, these columns frame views of the North Newport River where a ferry landing once provided crossings for travelers on Georgia's oldest road.

39

Inspired by the shape of a nineteenth-century dining room in Savannah, a curved wall accommodates a china cabinet in one corner of the room and a triangular antechamber leads to the kitchen in another.

The kitchen recalls the appearance of an old-fashioned keeping room—a place where food was kept warm after it was brought in from the cookhouse. Reclaimed boards planed by hand more than a century ago cover the walls and ceiling of the room, glowing warmly in

the light of an antique gasolier. In shades ranging from pale gray to deep reddish brown, they form a rustic backdrop for the room's simple cabinetry and cozy sitting area.

In contrast, finely milled cypress paneling covers the walls of the library, where the homeowner conducts business while in residence. Like plantation owners a century ago, he can look through the windows and see anyone coming from a mile away or step through a double-hung window to catch a breeze on the porch. The master bedroom behind the library has an equally expansive view, overlooking the river where a ferry once carried travelers across the water.

LEFT AND ABOVE: *In the central living hall, two pairs of doors with working transoms and Greek Revival tapered architraves lead to the four rooms that flank it. With front and back doors, double-hung windows tall enough to walk through onto the porch, and a pair of working fireplaces, the symmetrically arranged room is inviting in all seasons.*

In the dining room, delicate pilasters frame a built-in china cabinet and murals that depict the Lowcountry landscape. Inspired by the scenic wallpaper popular on both sides of the Atlantic in the eighteenth and nineteenth centuries, the murals marry natural and historic detail. The fine craftsmanship of the room's curved walls and moldings recalls the artisanship of nineteenth-century master carpenters who built lavish rooms for Southern plantation houses.

The ferry is long gone, but a 1928 mahogany sports-fisherman boat moors at a dock, where it serves as an unusual guest suite. More guest quarters are housed nearby in a structure resembling an old oyster factory. Raised high like the main house, its upper floor shades a ground-level platform where oysters might have been shucked and cotton stored before being shipped to nearby Savannah. Today, this area provides a sheltered place for games and entertaining, while the upper floors accommodate a gathering space and sleeping quarters for visitors.

Built with pine beams in true timber-frame construction, the guesthouse provides a perfect counterpoint to the cultivated beauty of the main house. While one captures the sturdy simplicity of post-and-beam carpentry, the other celebrates the elegance of Greek Revival design. Shaped by the region's vernacular architecture, both high and low, the buildings offer tribute to the past. Like the South's great plantations, they also pay homage to place—to the rich history of the site, the beauty of the land, and the power of the river that runs through it.

LEFT: *Dry-docked on the edge of the river, a 1928 mahogany boat was transformed into unusual guest quarters that invite visitors to enjoy the tranquil setting. A simple screened building behind it is a popular spot for oyster roasts and barbecues.* BELOW: *In the large guesthouse, walls of windows and doors open to a wraparound porch. Guests sleep in small bedrooms on a loft level and share breakfast in the gathering room below.*

The form of the guesthouse recalls early waterfront structures such as oyster factories and storehouses for indigo, rice, and other agricultural products. Built in true post-and-beam construction, it employs the same mortise-and-tenon joinery common to eighteenth- and nineteenth-century structures.

Cottage Revisited

PALMETTO BLUFF, SOUTH CAROLINA

O n a visit to Saint Simons Island in Georgia, I took a side trip to the nearby town of Brunswick. In this quintessential small Southern town, nineteenth- and early twentieth-century houses sit side by side on streets shaded by oak trees and magnolias. In towns like these, I notice how the homes work together to create a vibrant and engaging streetscape. And I often find myself captivated by a single house, which by virtue of its simplicity, honest craftsmanship, perfect proportions, and quirky details, stands out from the rest.

A cottage caught my eye in a Brunswick neighborhood where I imagined generations of shrimpers and stevedores living simply along the coast. The little one-story building had a single dormer, a tin roof, and a deep front porch with canvas curtains hanging from its corners for privacy. Comfortable and inviting, yet also veiled from view, this was a porch you could enjoy spending time on. Even though I never set foot inside the modest cottage, I could easily envision the simple materials and carpentry within.

Several years later, when designing my beach house in WaterColor, Florida, the memory of this cottage returned. Unlike that cottage, this would be a vacation retreat, but our needs were much the same—finding shelter from the elements, communing with neighbors, and enjoying time with family and friends. Many of the cottage's details found their way into our house, from the tin roof and dormer window to the porch's pierced slats and curtains. Inside, I created the simple floor plan and interiors I had seen with my mind's eye, with distressed wood floors, painted wood walls, old lighting, and plain trim.

Five years later, my Brunswick-born beach cottage became the inspiration for another home, this time in the new coastal community of Palmetto Bluff in South Carolina. Intended to complement the Southern vernacular character of the streetscape, the new cottage also needed to reflect the relaxed refinement of the community.

RIGHT: *Surrounded by pierced slat railings and louvered shutters, the front porch of this coastal cottage is a comfortable outdoor living room to be enjoyed in all weather.* OVERLEAF: *While the house's corrugated metal roof, central dormer, and deep porch are hallmarks of Southern coastal cottages, the row of French doors reflects a Caribbean influence. When they are open, the porch becomes an outdoor extension of the main interior living space.*

A marble-topped island separates the kitchen from the dining and living area. Along the front of the house, French doors connect these spaces to the porch. When the porch shutters are closed and doors opened, the entire front of the house becomes a large, indoor-outdoor space for living and entertaining.

LEFT: *In this bedroom, a ladder-style door, painted wood walls, and simple antiques recall the cozy bedrooms of old-fashioned Southern cottages.* ABOVE: *With stairs climbing to a bunkroom beneath the slope of the hipped roof, a hallway leads to first-floor bedrooms and a spacious back porch. Although it is an interior space, the hall is illuminated by shared light coming through transoms above the front and rear doors.*

Like the old house in Brunswick, the new cottage greets guests with a deep front porch just steps away from the sidewalk, but louvered shutters replace the canvas curtains for a more sophisticated first impression. Inside, the interior designer struck an upscale-down-South balance by juxtaposing Greek Revival pilasters with walls of painted cypress boards. In the kitchen, marble countertops sit atop simple yet elegant, well-crafted cabinetry. Painted cypress boards cover all but one wall in the master bedroom, where built-in closets and cabinets with mirrored doors offer a degree of luxury not usually found in early Southern cottages.

Through this process of revisiting and reinterpreting the old cottage in Brunswick, I realized that it is a building-block house. You can dress it up or dress it down. You can take something away or add something new. The details change to suit the setting and the taste of the inhabitants, but the basic shape remains the same, because it meets the canons of great comfort. A straightforward building designed for comfortable family living, it is a Southern archetype that transcends time—and even place.

LEFT: *Opening directly to the rear porch, the master bathroom features a marble floor and countertop that provide a refined counterpoint to beadboard walls and simple trim.* ABOVE: *With uncomplicated trim and transom-like upper panels, the expanse of built-in closets and cabinets complements the master bedroom's simple painted plank walls. Although the overall mood of the blue-and-white room is casual, the mirrored and curtained closet doors and dark brown accents add hints of sophistication.*

ABOVE AND RIGHT: *A screened porch spanning the rear of the house is another place to gather and relax. Canvas curtains inspired by the cottage in Brunswick provide privacy and protection from the elements. A brick fireplace offers wintertime warmth for the small dining area at one end of the porch, and a hanging daybed at its other end is the perfect place to nap beneath the exposed corrugated metal roof.*

Lowcountry Federal

SPRING ISLAND, SOUTH CAROLINA

When clients asked us to design a house on Spring Island overlooking the tidal marshes of Chechessee Creek, we did not need to look far for inspiration. The bluff at the water's edge reminded us of the earliest settlement in nearby Beaufort, where eighteenth- and nineteenth-century houses cluster on a point of land surrounded by the Beaufort River. Typically built in the shape of a *T* to maximize cross ventilation, these houses have wide, formal façades that face the street. Behind them, narrow wings extend toward the water, wrapped with porches where residents enjoy breezes and river views.

Like many of these Beaufort-style dwellings, this house is Federal in style, but with a less formal Lowcountry accent. The side-gabled roof, central entrance crowned by an elliptical fanlight, and five bays of symmetrically spaced windows are all classic Federal elements. To these we added variations, widening and deepening what would have been a small portico to create an inviting Southern porch with a graceful split stair.

Illuminated by the front door's fanlight, the center hall has a strong Federal character. Upon entering, you instantly become aware of the simple beauty of the staircase's turned newel post and gracefully curved rail. Historically accurate in style and craftsmanship, the rail was constructed from blocks of heart pine that local woodworkers cut, shaped, and rasped exactly as their predecessors did in the early days of Beaufort.

In contrast to the stair's elegance, the walls are clad in painted buttboard, introducing a more casual style. This juxtaposition of the formal with the informal recalls the wall treatments of an old plantation house outside Beaufort on St. Helena Island. Such combinations of high and low style can be found in many Beaufort houses, where a mix of Federal, Greek Revival, and indigenous details tells the story of changing tastes and fortunes.

In the Beaufort tradition, this classic five-bay Federal-style house is modified with flanking wings set back from the central façade to improve cross ventilation. The simple details of the wings recede from the more highly decorated primary façade, where a porch with Tuscan columns, square pilasters, and an elliptical fanlight draw attention to the center of the house.

LEFT: *In the entrance hall, walls of vertically and horizontally applied buttboard reflect Lowcountry vernacular methods of building with simple carpentry and local materials like pine and cypress boards. Curving from the first to second floor with no intermediate support, the more refined stair rail creates a graceful silhouette.* OVERLEAF: *Square columns and a wide cross beam separate the living room from the sitting and dining rooms beyond, which were designed to resemble an enclosed porch.*

This approach is most evident in this house's living room, where Greek Revival columns and a Federal-style mantel contrast with painted pine buttboard surfaces. More modern in plan than nineteenth-century rooms, this living area flows into the adjacent rooms. At one end, a curtain wall with a large pass-through into the kitchen allows family and friends to interact with each other across the spaces. Fitted with large shutters, the pass-through can easily be closed to screen the kitchen from view when the residents entertain.

Both the living room and kitchen open to a glassed veranda surrounded by marshland and river views. Although the original plans called for this area to be an open-air porch, our clients wanted enclosed living and entertaining spaces overlooking the landscape. Returning to Beaufort and other coastal towns for inspiration, we looked at old photographs and even peered through hedges to study the way past generations had enclosed porches to increase interior space.

Inspired by vernacular Lowcountry houses, this residence testifies to their beauty, adaptability, and functionality. Capturing their essence, it also demonstrates the timeless wisdom of those who built and lived in them.

A partition wall inspired by old-fashioned breakfronts divides the living room from the kitchen. With double-hinged, louvered shutters, the pass-through opens wide for ease of communication between the rooms. While the style of the house is traditional, the open flow among the living and entertaining spaces is more relaxed and modern in spirit.

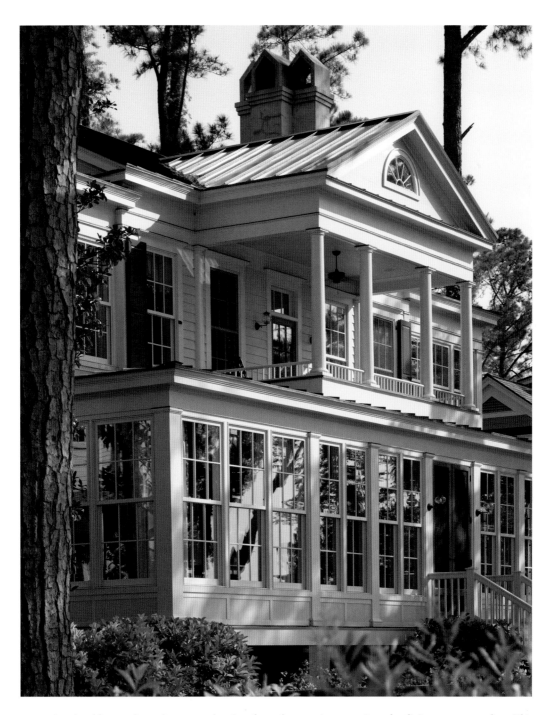

LEFT: *A pair of louvered panels screens the view from the morning room into the dining room next door. This opening mirrors the French doors that lead to a screened porch on the far side of the dining room.* ABOVE: *Closely spaced, double-hung windows line the walls of the rear rooms, recalling those traditionally used to enclose porches in Beaufort. Although the Federal portico adds a formal element to the riverside façade, the expanse of windows on its lower level contributes a more relaxed appearance.*

North Meets South

BRIDGEHAMPTON, NEW YORK

Traveling down a lane bordered by dense green hedges, you have every reason to believe that it leads to a charming old house. When you arrive at its end, you are not disappointed. On the far side of a wooden gate stands a traditional cedar-shake-shingled house with white trim and black shutters that looks just like the other old houses you passed on the way. The only difference is that this one was built in the twenty-first century.

When asked to design a house in Bridgehampton, we sent a team to tour New England and the Mid-Atlantic states. Although a Southern firm, we have long been interested in Northeastern architecture and its influence below the Mason-Dixon line. There was a wealth of inspiration to be found for this project in the vernacular dwellings of the Hamptons and the whalers' cottages of Nantucket.

We also took cues from the site—a gently sloping field once farmed for potatoes. Surrounded by old estates, the new house needed to appear as if it belonged in their midst. With a barn on one side and a saltbox-style cottage on the other, the four-bay gabled house resembles the home of a thriving farmer. Although these buildings would have been spread apart in a true farmstead, we brought them together and joined them, creating a single dwelling that seems to ramble a bit over the land where it stands.

Like so many Bridgehampton houses, the main structure has an understated façade, with the exception of the front door, which makes a strong first impression. Crowned with a Neoclassical portico, it is framed by latticework pilasters reminiscent of the rose-covered lattices of Nantucket. In between these, an antique English pine door opens into a small room known locally as a cold room. More functional than ornamental, it is a place to escape the weather when taking off boots and hanging up coats.

RIGHT: *With flowering vines growing over the window's trellis, this small wing calls to mind the little rose-covered whalers' cottages of Nantucket.* OVERLEAF: *Paying homage to the architectural traditions of the Northeast, this home's enclosed portico, six-over-six windows, weathered shingles, white trim, and black shutters resemble Federal, Colonial Revival, and Shingle-style houses throughout the region.*

Yankee thrift is a trait associated with this region—often a necessity for farmers and whalers who worked hard to survive in the harsh climate. In domestic architecture, this translates into simple, comfortable houses with modest decoration and an economical use of the space. These attributes find full expression in the house's great room, where walls are trimmed with plain moldings and a low ceiling and large hearth recall the days when wood-burning fires were the only source of heat. Every space in the room is used to the fullest, including the wall beside the fireplace, where strap-hinge cabinets provide storage for logs and household items.

LEFT: *Although the ceilings are low in the great room, in keeping with eighteenth- and nineteenth-century proportions, light blue walls with crisp white trim brighten the space. Spare in style, the brick fireplace does not call attention to itself with an elaborate mantel.* ABOVE: *Unlike the rest of the house's small, cozy rooms, the master bedroom has a high ceiling and large windows with views of the garden.*

In the breakfast room, a row of double-hung windows overlooks the garden. More windows and a door open to a porch that provides outdoor dining and living areas. Instead of crown moldings, a simple ledge surrounds the room, providing a place to display a collection of antique bottles.

The small staircase behind the fireplace is another expression of the region's judicious use of space. Instead of a grand stair hall, it is tucked into a narrow vestibule that leads to the study and master bedroom located in the saltbox-style wing. The kitchen is on the other side of the great room. Floor-to-ceiling cabinets on two walls provide ample storage space for tableware, pots and pans, and dry goods. A small breakfast room next door is just large enough for a cozy banquette tucked beneath the windows and a table with four chairs.

One of our favorite parts of the house—perhaps because it so completely captures the region's quirks—is a passage full of twists and turns and tight staircases that opens off the breakfast room. Leading to doors in both the front and back of the house, it includes a mudroom at ground level, a laundry and powder room on the main floor, and stairs to the guest suite above the garage. Though small and compressed, all the spaces are used to full capacity.

This same approach is evident in the guest suite squeezed beneath the garage's barn-style roof. A bedroom just bigger than the bed within it fills the area underneath one gable. A kitchenette occupies a second gable, and a bathroom, the third. The largest space in the suite is a central sitting area designed with grandchildren in mind. Flooded with light from a cupola in the ceiling, the room opens to the back of the house with French doors and a balcony.

While the front of the house is old Bridgehampton in style, we gave way to Southern frivolity on the back with large expanses of windows and a porch that invites you to sit down and relax. Perhaps because we have Southern roots, we believe that no house is complete without a porch. While revisiting the Northeastern styles that influence so much of our work, we couldn't resist adding a Southern accent in the end.

LEFT AND BELOW: *Fitted beneath the carriage house roof, this tiny guest suite exemplifies the region's efficient use of space. A bathroom with a space-saving sliding door, an alcove kitchenette, and a sleeping loft just big enough for a double mattress open off the small sitting area in the center. Shining down through a cupola and in through French doors and gable windows, sunlight reflects against glossy white ceilings.*

Seen from the lush gardens at the rear of the home, the carriage house clearly resembles an old barn attached to the main house by a breezeway. This breezeway merges seamlessly into the spacious back porch, which serves as a seasonal outdoor living room. The roof's long dormer window is drawn from vernacular examples.

Designed by Nature

SPRING ISLAND, SOUTH CAROLINA

Coastal houses from the Outer Banks of North Carolina to the Florida Keys, and as far afield as the Caribbean, share many common features—raised foundations, pitched roofs, large windows with storm shutters, generous verandas or porches. From region to region, there is also tremendous individuality. Shutters can be top-hinged or side-hinged, solid or louvered, decorated or plain. Roofs can be gabled or hipped and covered with tin, shingles, or thatch. The variations are endless, reflecting the builders' response to the same elements—sun, heat, wind, and tides—and the question of how best to live in harmony with them.

Borrowing freely from this global palette, we designed a house on the tidal marshes of Spring Island that is an eclectic and original response to its setting. Set far back on a dirt road and shielded from neighboring properties by thick curtains of trees and undergrowth, the site had an almost primeval aura. In such an unspoiled wilderness, it was essential that the house sit lightly on the land, with as little impact on its surroundings as possible.

Like many coastal cottages, the house is long, one story tall, and mostly one room deep. Rising above potential floodwaters on wood pilings, it floats over the landscape, inviting breezes to flow beneath its floor. The structure of the house is simple, covered by a continuous hipped roof with deep overhangs that shelter it on all four sides. Supported by large X-shaped braces, the overhangs shade front and back porches and protect the interior from sun and rain. On either side of the front porch, tall Bermuda shutters hinged at the top open like awnings to filter the elements further.

Shaded by the porches and cooled naturally by cross ventilation, a long great room forms the core of the house. Constructed in the age-old timber-frame method, massive beams and trusses made of cedar support its cypress walls and ceiling. The scent and burnished patina of the wood recalls old Cuban and Bermudian villas, which were commonly built of cedar and mahogany.

Louvered Bermuda shutters and the metal roof's deep overhang shade the cottage's porches and rooms from the bright coastal sun. Clerestory windows in wide dormers spanning the roof bring diffuse illumination into the house.

ABOVE: *When combined, traditional coastal details including pulley-operated Bermuda shutters and scissor trusses contribute a subtle sense of drama to the cottage's façade.* RIGHT: *On the rear of the house, a wide screened porch flanked by the master bedroom suite and a guest bedroom overlook the Colleton River.*

A wall of French doors inspired by West Indian plantations dissolves the barrier between the great room and the view of the marsh and creek behind the house. Folding open, the doors leave nothing but a framework of pine posts and beams to separate the great room from the back porch and landscape beyond. Occupying one-third of the house's square footage, the porch has the inviting charm of an outside room where families relax throughout the day, enjoying their surroundings and each other's company.

The design of the house accentuates its openness to light, air, and the landscape. Large windows illuminate every room, including the master bathroom, where a freestanding tub is tucked into a bay window that frames the landscape. Louvered shutters divide the master

The great room that forms the core of the cottage features a timber-frame skeleton of twelve-by-twelve-inch cedar beams. Its rustic simplicity belies the skilled artistry of the mortise-and-tenon joinery. Light from the porch shines through the French doors and transoms to glow against the unstained wood, which will age to a rich, mellow patina over time.

bedroom and guest room from the porch, sliding shut for privacy while still allowing coastal breezes to ventilate the rooms.

Inspired by the wisdom of coastal cottages from around the world, the house works in harmony with its surroundings. Protecting inhabitants from the elements, it also unites them with the land, inviting them to enjoy the power and beauty of nature from a place of shelter and comfort.

LEFT: *Multiple species of wood, such as heart pine floors, pine beams, and cypress boards, are used throughout the great room, including this dining area.* ABOVE: *The clerestory windows of the wide front dormer illuminate the kitchen. Double-sided cabinetry serving both the kitchen and the great room creates partial separation between the spaces while affording the kitchen a view to the marsh behind the house.*

Mahogany French doors open from the great room and master bedroom to the back porch. Measuring more than twelve hundred square feet, the porch offers a sheltered outdoor living space from which to enjoy the natural surroundings. Light slants in through the rear dormer, passing through clerestory windows into the adjoining great room.

SOUL OF PLACE

A house that is at home
in its setting resonates
with timeless authenticity
and creates an atmosphere
of comfort and belonging.

THE HUMAN EXPERIENCE OF PLACE is as subtle as the subconscious emotions we feel when we enter a home or as direct as the pleasure of discovering a beautiful view. By coaxing each site into revealing its assets, whether the curve of a river, a canopy of old oaks, or the character of the neighboring houses, we invite it to teach us how best to express this sense of place. Beginning with careful consideration of what already exists on the physical site, the design process ideally ends with a house that will endure long after we are gone, offering future generations a strong sense of belonging and of coming home.

To respect their surroundings, buildings must also respond in form and style to the area's cultural heritage and architectural traditions. When creating cabins and a dining hall for Balsam Mountain Preserve in the Blue Ridge Mountains, we spent days driving through the surrounding mountains, touring old houses and agrarian structures. Constructed with authentic materials, many salvaged from the area, our buildings drew directly from the regional vernacular, right down to the rusty roofs. The result was a new retreat with all the rustic appeal of an old mountain community.

While the South is filled with vernacular traditions, it is also rich with refined cities where Classical styles find expression. People who walk down the streets of Charleston almost always notice the city's elegance and charm. However, they may not realize how the diversity of styles and building materials or the intimacy of the narrow side streets contribute to its appeal. The city is full of surprises and idiosyncrasies, especially when compared to Savannah's far more orderly arrangement of squares. Even within Savannah's plan, however, there is variety in scale, style, and the way the buildings relate to the sidewalks and streets. The character of old cities and towns like these inspires our work as "place makers" of new communities rooted in cultural heritage and geography.

When creating the architecture of a new main street, as we did in Palmetto Bluff, South Carolina, we respected both the beauty of the landscape and the region's urban traditions. We also paid attention to the ways buildings work together, not only with their surroundings but also as collections of structures serving a community. In Palmetto Bluff's village center, the main street parallels a village green dotted with old oak trees to terminate at the edge of a river. At the street's end, a corner store addresses the water with unusually wide windows inspired by an old store in a nearby village. Recalling familiar Southern streetscapes, the deep overhangs of the buildings create a porch-like walkway beneath which residents gather to enjoy each other's company and the surrounding views.

Whether designing individual homes or the architecture of entire communities, the process is the same. We start by analyzing the character of the land, the heritage of the region, and the vision of the client. By paying attention to both the spirit and specifics of place, we define a modern palette that speaks to each design's origins. The magic comes when you put them together to express the complex soul of a place.

PAGE 93: *The uncomplicated architecture of this back porch provides an ideal setting from which to enjoy the ever-changing vista of a South Carolina tidal marsh.* ABOVE: *Designed to resemble a house built by a local carpenter with materials harvested from the surrounding forest, this cottage retreat in Callaway Gardens is a quiet complement to the wooded Georgia setting.*

Making Place

PALMETTO BLUFF, SOUTH CAROLINA

When we were invited to establish the architectural foundations of the new community of Palmetto Bluff, the natural beauty of the site combined with the charm of the region's architectural traditions was inspirational. On a sea island south of Beaufort, South Carolina, Palmetto Bluff is surrounded by three rivers and laden with old oak trees, some more than a hundred years old. When the developers, Crescent Resources, and land planners, Hart Howerton, laid out the new town, they considered each one of the ancient trees sacred. Every aspect of the development—the roads, the sidewalks, the houses, the green spaces, the buildings—were fitted in among the trees, allowing the native landscape to pass its character on to the community.

"Place-making" is about having the eyes to see what already exists—the landscape, the old trees and rivers, the spirit of a place. We began by studying small coastal towns in the area, including Bluffton, where Palmetto Bluff is located. Rooted in more than two centuries of history and culture, Bluffton has been called the last true coastal village of the South. As we explored its houses, gardens, and commercial buildings, the simplicity of the architecture and the warmth of its small-town spirit were evident. We also toured Brunswick, Georgia; Beaufort, South Carolina; and Frogmore, a village on nearby St. Helena Island. All shared pedestrian-friendly downtowns with buildings in varied styles and scale and intimate residential neighborhoods.

Every small town has a place to shop and place to worship, so our main street design began with a general store on a prominent corner across the street from a one-room church. The store occupies a three-story building with a colonnade inspired by a streetscape in downtown Oxford, Mississippi. Addressing both the river and the street, it reaches over the sidewalk like a porch, offering a place for people to congregate beneath its shade.

A covered sidewalk inspired by main street architecture in old Southern towns invites pedestrians to relax beneath its shade. At one end of the sidewalk, a small chapel stands at the water's edge.

While the buildings on the main street vary in scale and style, they create a unified appearance when viewed across the village green. With a corner store, offices, and a modest post office, the block recalls the mix of buildings commonly found along main streets of countless small towns across America. The brick-paved street provides another touch of nostalgic texture to Palmetto Bluff's town center.

98

The town's residents also gather when collecting their mail at the post office next door, which is less than half the size of its immediate neighbors. Built in the Italianate manner popular for late nineteenth- and early twentieth-century governmental buildings, the post office also varies in style from its neighbors, reflecting the pluralism characteristic of old downtowns. Formal elements including the façade's parapet and the classical entablature within give the small building a sense of dignity. Balancing this, a simple shed-roof porch adds relaxed rural character, as well as a place to escape the sun.

The Carpenter Gothic–inspired chapel at the head of the village provides a different kind of communal space. The soul of the town, it is a favorite location for weddings, concerts, and lectures. From inside the short steeple, the church bell rings on the hour and the half hour, keeping time for the whole community. Perched on the edge of the May River, the church is fitted with triple-hung windows that open to the surrounding landscape. Equipped with mahogany screens that slide into pockets, the windows offer full exposure to the coastal climate during temperate months.

Beyond the village buildings, a residential neighborhood fans out in a crescent formed by a bend in the river. The streetscape resembles the architecture of early twentieth-century automobile suburbs, where individual houses of shared heritage reflect the particularity of homeowners and builders. As early as the late nineteenth century, builders consulted pattern books when designing houses, emulating their designs while adding their own innovations. Over time, many of these houses were modified as homeowners enlarged or altered them. The resulting neighborhoods are characterized not by homogeneity but a harmonious eclecticism that reveals the passage of time and the evolution of a community.

CLOCKWISE, FROM TOP LEFT: *Complete with reproduction bronze mailboxes, the interior of the post office is appropriately dignified. Inspired by rural Southern churches built before modern lighting and air-conditioning, the chapel maximizes natural light and cross ventilation with tall, clear windows fitted with sliding screens. Although its steeple and bell can be seen and heard throughout the village, the chapel assumes a humble presence beneath centuries-old live oaks. Board-and-batten shutters protect the chapel from coastal storms.*

Many of the houses in Palmetto Bluff's first residential neighborhood draw from patterns that we developed. Modified with varied porches, wings, and outbuildings, no two are alike. Thanks to the variety in the houses and the irregularities of the setbacks—dictated by the location of the old trees—the streets have a fortuitous charm. These are the things that give neighborhoods a genuine atmosphere.

It's challenging to create a new community that feels as though it has existed a long time. Places usually take many years to evolve. The best way to create the impression of time's passage is to embrace imperfection and idiosyncrasy. Idiosyncrasy is part of the randomness and peculiarity of place and time. If you can tap into that, the results are magical.

Old oak trees line the streets of Palmetto Bluff, where houses sit close to the sidewalk, as they did in turn-of-the-nineteenth-century neighborhoods. Shady, brick-paved sidewalks uninterrupted by driveways encourage strollers to greet their neighbors and enjoy one another's gardens. Modestly sized houses in unpretentious vernacular styles create a congenial streetscape, and gas street lanterns cast a warm, flickering glow.

Among the Oaks

SPRING ISLAND, SOUTH CAROLINA

The four massive live oaks that stand on this site have a strong but quiet presence. Establishing themselves as the centerpiece of the design, they taught us how to act in their presence and what shape the house and its outbuildings should take. Before beginning the design process, we commissioned an extensive tree survey, studying their roots, limbs, and canopy in order to build respectfully among them.

Within this setting, the clients envisioned a relaxed, informal house. Enamored of the openness, natural materials, and unassuming silhouette of Caribbean architecture, they asked us to incorporate these things in the design. By combining their vision with elements from nearby Lowcountry plantations, we created a design that could be equally at home in South Carolina and the Caribbean. In our imagination, the house resembled something that an eighteenth-century British planter might have built after settling in South Carolina following a sojourn in the West Indies.

In keeping with traditional Southern plantation style, the house stands on handmade brick steps that ascend to a gracious veranda. Instead of the central, solid wood door one would expect to find, however, a series of glass-and-mahogany French doors with shutters reminiscent of West Indies plantations span the façade. Like many West Indian dwellings, the house is one story high with the exception of a lantern that pierces the low-pitched roof to accommodate a treetop sanctuary within. While the lantern is atypical of Southern design, most of the building materials, including the standing-seam metal roof, handmade brick, and tabby, are indigenous.

This interplay of styles and materials continues inside, where the core of the house is a spacious, airy room facing both the front and back of the property. The form of this pavilion-like space resembles the interior of a Caribbean plantation, but the walls are embellished with classical elements recalling traditional Lowcountry style. Because the pilasters, columns,

An iron gate is the entryway to a compound where massive oak trees rise high enough to spread their branches above the surrounding buildings. Sheltered by a double-hipped metal roof and deep porches, the primary residence opens to the enveloping landscape.

Encircling the oaks, the compound includes a two-bedroom guesthouse, the main residence, which combines communal spaces with the master bedroom suite, and a carriage house with a garage, a home office, and an additional guest room. This collection of varied buildings merges organically into its unspoiled natural setting.

ABOVE: *A spiral stair leads to a small room with a 360-degree view located within the lantern that rises above the house's roof.* RIGHT: *Simultaneously rustic and sophisticated, the great room combines a West Indian–inspired ceiling of exposed beams and purlins combined with columns, pilasters, and a tall entablature. Because they are constructed of painted wood instead of plaster, the Classical elements have an understated elegance that complements the room's natural wood and brick surfaces.* OVERLEAF: *With the French doors open, the back porch becomes an open-air extension of the great room.*

and architrave are expressed in simple Greek Revival style, as though fashioned by a country carpenter, they complement the primitive Caribbean-style ceiling of exposed rafters, purlins, and textured surfaces.

The outbuildings quote Southern vernacular style more directly by drawing inspiration from utilitarian buildings on working plantations. We emulated plantation workers' cottages for the guesthouse, altering the floor plan to accommodate the two massive oaks that split the site. Resolving the problem by dividing the buildings into two seemingly separate cottages, we connected them with a narrow breezeway that squeezes between the tree trunks.

ABOVE: *Beyond the kitchen, a sitting room occupies an airy bay with windows on three sides and French doors that open to the back porch.* RIGHT: *Across the front of the house, shallow steps of Savannah gray brick descend to a veranda paved in tabby, a concrete made from crushed shells and lime that has been used in the Lowcountry for centuries.*

Inspired by simple workers' quarters on Southern plantations, the guesthouse has many classic Southern vernacular details: standing-seam metal roofs, white clapboard walls, shed-roof porches sheltering doors with transoms, and a large screen porch. The two front doors open to separate one-bedroom suites where guests can enjoy privacy.

A carriage house with large barn doors and a lantern atop its roof stands across from the guesthouse. Accommodating a family room and a second-floor guest room and office, it contributes more space to the compound without adding mass to the main house. Facing the guesthouse, the carriage house forms an enclosure around the shaded lawn of native ground-cover in front of the house. Like the oaks that have stood on the property for more than a century, the buildings define a receiving room for the entire compound, creating a welcoming embrace. In the words of the homeowner, as soon as you pass through the front gate, you enter into the heart of the house.

LEFT AND ABOVE: *In the morning kitchen that connects the two guest suites, painted buttboard walls and a tongue-and-groove ceiling create a comfortable atmosphere of informality. Simple cabinetry, a farmhouse sink, heart pine countertops, and a plate rack with distressed beadboard backing impart more rural charm. The room's long, narrow shape, wall-to-wall windows, and exposed rafters recall the open-air breezeways that inspired it.*

Waterscape

SPRING ISLAND, SOUTH CAROLINA

What's most striking about this waterfront dwelling is the way that it does *not* strike you at once with its presence. Upon approaching it, you don't immediately encounter a single building. Instead, you engage directly with the landscape that surrounds it. With no dominant façade or obvious front door, the compound's centerpiece is a breezeway that frames a vista of an old oak tree and the river beyond. Only after entering its shade do you find the front door and come inside the house.

The beauty of the natural setting shaped the compound's form. Located on the banks of the Colleton River, the site was chosen by a Chicago family desiring a closer connection to nature. Their requirements included water views from as many rooms as possible; porches, balconies, and terraces where they could bask in the Lowcountry surroundings; and separate guest quarters for visiting family and friends.

The compound's buildings include four modestly sized structures linked by porches and breezeways. Paralleling the river, the main dwelling and two guesthouses overlook it with screened porches and balconies. With white clapboard walls and louvered shutters, they recall the simple houses of the rural South. Built in the style of a barn, the fourth structure completes the compound's resemblance to an old family farm. When approached by land, the string of buildings invites you to look and walk right through it. From the river, it's camouflaged beneath a canopy of oaks and Spanish moss.

This unity with the landscape continues within, where nearly every room has a direct view of the river. In the main house, the river's sparkling light dances on the ceiling of a dining room tucked into a bay where three walls of windows frame a panoramic view. Diffuse light bathes the living room, where glazed doors open to a screened porch overlooking the waterway and windows set high in the ceiling offer glimpses of clouds and sky.

A series of breezeways and porches connect the main house on the left with two guesthouses and a third outbuilding on the right. Thanks to the temperate climate, these spaces form an outdoor hallway inviting residents and their guests to engage with the surrounding landscape.

This compound is a rambling array of interconnected small buildings. The cottage-like structure on the left is in actuality a wing of the main house. Resembling a barn, the building on the right includes a large recreation room, guest quarters, and storage for garden tools and boating and fishing equipment.

LEFT: *Parallel to one of the guesthouses, this porch overlooks a courtyard in front of the compound. Although it serves as a covered walkway to the main house, the porch is wide enough for sitting and relaxing in comfortable wicker furniture.* ABOVE: *In the living room, gable and dormer windows bring in light that glows against the warm, rich tones of the ceiling's salvaged pine planks and beams. French doors on either side of the fireplace open to a porch overlooking the river.*

ABOVE AND RIGHT: *Illuminated by a large metal-framed skylight, vestiges of white paint give the kitchen's ceiling a soft patina. The long marble-topped kitchen island is ideal both for cooking and enjoying an informal meal. One step down from the kitchen, the dining room literally descends into the landscape that surrounds it.*

Throughout the main house, salvaged building materials call to mind the texture and forms of rural architecture. In the living room, massive beams and trusses of reclaimed heart pine support a soaring ceiling covered with wide pine boards. In the kitchen and master bedroom, antique planks of wood with vestiges of old paint add rustic patina. Although the wood in the guesthouses is newly milled, the buttboard walls and tongue-and-groove ceilings recall old-fashioned building materials and styles.

Unlike the guesthouse walls, nearly every surface and support in the barn-style building is made from reclaimed wood. Gathered from old barns, boards of varying widths cover the floors, walls, ceilings, and stair treads, and weathered beams with splintered ends serve as newel posts. Although many people might consider such materials to be useless relics, our clients had the wisdom to recognize their value.

LEFT: *In one of the guesthouses, a breakfast room is tucked into a bay window that overlooks the river. A pale blue tongue-and-groove ceiling and three walls of windows give it a porch-like atmosphere.* ABOVE: *Among the compound's many indoor-outdoor spaces, this screened porch paralleling the living room is the largest. Wrapped on three sides with screens, cooled by ceiling fans, and warmed in wintertime by a brick fireplace, the wicker-furnished space is a year-round open-air living room.*

In the end, the magic of this compound comes from the synthesis of many factors—the materials, the setting, the clients' vision. When they enjoy time with family and friends, filling up the rooms, relaxing on the porches, or heading out to the boat dock for a fishing expedition, the place comes alive.

LEFT: *Inspired by antique barns, this building provides a rustic retreat for reading, tying fishing ties, and listening to and playing music. A ladder leads to a sleeping area tucked in a hayloft-style space between the barnlike room's salvaged wood ceiling.* ABOVE: *In the guest bedroom, a built-in wardrobe and bunk equipped with drawers, all made of recycled barn wood, make the most of the small space.*

ABOVE: *Throughout the barnlike building's rooms, salvaged boards of random widths and finishes cover the walls, floors, and ceilings and are used in the staircase and cabinetry.* RIGHT: *Against this backdrop, a shower with glass doors and gleaming blue tiles adds pleasing contrast and a modern note.* OVERLEAF: *Viewed from the river, the compound's silhouette of rambling, interrelated buildings resembles a group of separate, closely spaced houses.*

House on a Hill

S urrounded by old oaks and Georgia pines, native azaleas and heirloom roses, bountiful vegetable gardens, horse paddocks, and acres of green fields, this rambling farmhouse looks as though it has stood on this knoll for generations. When the homeowners first purchased the farm, however, the only building on the hilltop site was a decades-old prefabricated home. Although utilitarian at best, it still became a cherished family retreat.

After spending weekends in the prefab house for many years, our clients decided to make the farm their permanent residence. Realizing that the small house could not meet their everyday needs, they commissioned a country home befitting of a Southern horse farm. After selecting a site for the new house at the bottom of the knoll, we set to work on designs.

Meanwhile, the clients moved full-time into the little house on the hill, improving it with the goal of turning it into a guesthouse. The more time they spent there, the more they realized that the original owners of the farm had been right when they located their house on top of the hill. Shaded by old trees and overlooking acres of rolling countryside, it was the most picturesque spot on the property. They came to the conclusion that it was the only place for their new house to be. The problem was that something was already there.

Leveling the house would have been the easy solution, but it also would have been reckless and wasteful. Although the ceilings were low and the rooms small, the house held many wonderful memories for the clients, their children, and grandchildren. So we did what generations of homeowners have done in the past: study the original house and ask, "How can we use this differently?"

The house's brown shingles and stone chimneys are a perfect foil for the old trees, sloping lawn, and naturalistic plantings of the bucolic setting.

The split-rail fence enclosing the rambling house and outbuildings, including a stable hidden beneath the trees, reinforces the impression of an old farm sitting atop a hill. Exterior walls of local stone and brown shingles and stone chimneys rising above the roofs unite the buildings with their natural surroundings.

Built on the footprint of the existing house, the new living and dining rooms have an open floor plan, higher ceilings, and walls of windows that contrast with the dark, cramped spaces of the original home. French doors from the dining room open to a dining porch with panoramic views and a stone fireplace.

From the beginning, the clients told us they imagined a home resembling a farmhouse that had grown over the years. This idea led to the solution of wrapping the original house with porches and rooms that appeared to have been added one by one. With a wide bay of windows, a screened porch with a tall stone chimney, and a long bedroom wing, the new façade bears little resemblance to the prefab house's plain face and small size.

Inside, we maintained the footprint of the original house's rooms as much as possible. Opening up the walls of the living and dining rooms, we still retained their cozy proportions. A new bay of windows in the living room makes space for a sitting area with a wide view of the lake. In the dining room, a wall of French doors and windows opens to a spacious porch, flooding the room with light. Pilasters and crown moldings contrast with buttboard walls and ceilings in both rooms, creating a style that is both casual and refined.

These rooms open off an entry hall that bridges the spaces of the original home with an addition three times its size. A large new kitchen with reclaimed pine floors that add the burnish of age opens to the front porch—an all-weather living space where wicker seating encircles a stone fireplace. This gathering space connects to the master suite with French doors and louvered pocket screens that allow the clients to enjoy fresh air without sacrificing privacy.

Inspired by love for a particular place, the house creates a strong connection with the landscape. Each room leads to a porch or commands a view across the rolling hills. With all the comforts of a modern home, it still feels like an old farmhouse shaped by the land on which it stands.

TOP: *Materials and details including brick and heart pine floors, wood walls, tall baseboards, and transoms create an atmosphere of refined country elegance.* LOWER RIGHT: *The light-colored walls and warm tones of the floors provide a perfect backdrop for the clients' collection of simple country antiques, prints, and transferware arranged throughout the house.* LOWER LEFT: *A bedroom for grandchildren recalls an old sleeping porch.*

LEFT: *Fieldstone fireplaces inside the house and on the porches create a warm and welcoming atmosphere through-out the seasons. Vintage-style wicker chairs and a table with an antique plank top add to the dining porch's atmo-sphere of relaxed hospitality.* ABOVE: *Although the shingles of the pool house roof contrast with the house's tin roof, the brown and white walls and stone chimneys visually unite them, contributing to a cohesive compound of buildings.*

Viewed from the side, the house clearly fulfills the clients' vision of a home resembling an old farmhouse that was added on to over the years. A more formal brick-and-boxwood garden softened by plantings of colorful flowers reflects the marriage of simple and sophisticated details found inside the house.

Mountaintop Retreat

SYLVA, NORTH CAROLINA

In the late nineteenth century, it was popular to summer at rustic mountain camps. With clusters of simple cabins in wilderness settings, retreats like the Great Camps of the Adirondacks allowed families to relax together and enjoy fresh air and spectacular views. Among the earliest examples of vernacular revival architecture, these buildings were constructed in local styles, with stones from nearby fields and logs and shingles cut from native trees. The founders of Balsam Mountain Preserve in the Blue Ridge Mountains asked us to design a collection of cabins and a dining hall that would recall the relaxed atmosphere of these havens.

The site for the enclave was a narrow ridge in the Great Balsam Mountains. On one side, it drops precipitously to a valley, providing a spectacular view of rolling mountains. Tall stands of hemlocks, locust trees, and tulip poplars provide a sense of shelter and protection from the wind. Nestled into this setting, ten cabins fan out on either side of a gravel road with the dining hall in the center. Surrounded by mature trees and shrubs that appear to have grown up around them, the cabins recede into the landscape.

The buildings of Balsam Mountain Preserve are deeply rooted in local architecture, revealing the influence of log cabins, plank barns, and humble houses built by the area's settlers. At the project's outset, the developer and a local contractor who salvages materials from nearby barns and houses led us on a tour of the region. An abandoned farmhouse with a rusty tin roof and walls made from sixteen-inch-wide boards of chestnut especially captured our imagination. The raw natural beauty of the materials conveyed a deep sense of integrity, and the building's spare, functional design spoke of the ingenuity and perseverance of those who built and lived in it.

Constructed of reclaimed wood, including boards of white oak, chestnut, poplar, and yellow pine, the cottages are built from the same materials that farmers in the surrounding mountains and valleys used more than a century ago. Even the rusty roofs sheltering the front doors and windows are made of metal salvaged from abandoned buildings in the area.

Locust trees like the one in the foreground were often used in timber-pole construction, as illustrated by this pair of cottages connected by a communal porch. Railings made from interwoven laurel branches demonstrate another traditional use of local building materials.

LEFT: *Although the walls of the sitting room and adjoining alcove bedroom are made of new pine planks, random widths and visible knots suggest that they are as old as the cottage's antique pine floorboards. Heavy salvaged beams add more texture and historic atmosphere to the cottage interiors.* ABOVE: *In the bathroom, planked sliding doors topped by operable transoms provide privacy for the shower and water closet.*

Inspired by primitive buildings like this, the cabins and dining hall at Balsam Mountain Preserve are constructed with the same materials and techniques. Old tin sheathing and boards of chestnut, poplar, and pine salvaged from nearby barns and houses offer the authentic patina of age. Stacked stone piers made with rocks from nearby mountains share the rugged craftsmanship of centuries past. Harking back to a traditional Blue Ridge Mountain style, porch posts and railings fashioned from the trunks of locust trees are interwoven with mountain laurel branches for decorative effect.

BELOW: *Inspired by the lodges of the Great Camps of the Adirondacks, the dining hall's central gathering space draws from vernacular building techniques, including timber-frame construction. Shaded by porches on three sides, the room is illuminated by dormer windows.* RIGHT: *Bark-covered timber poles, salvaged plank walls, and a ruggedly constructed fireplace of local stone connect the interior of this porch with its natural setting.*

With stone fireplaces and floorboards of salvaged heart-pine boards ranging from six to nineteen inches wide, the cabin interiors are as authentic as their façades. Recalling the economical use of space in rural architecture, each cabin has only two rooms, a central living area opening to a small bedroom alcove. On the rear of the cabins, which measure on average only six hundred square feet, large porches nearly double their space and serve as open-air living rooms. In some cases, porches connect two cabins, creating spacious quarters with both communal and private areas for families with children or friends vacationing together.

The dining hall that sits at the top of the ridge is the main gathering area. Designed to resemble an old barn repurposed for the camp's use, the building gives the impression of having been expanded over the years by generations of campgoers. In the large sitting room, high ceilings with reclaimed pine timbers and mortise-and-tenon joinery recall the sturdy construction of traditional agrarian structures. With walls of windows fitted between rugged posts, the long room that parallels this sitting area resembles a porch added to the barn and later enclosed to create an indoor dining room.

A true porch wraps the building on three sides, overlooking a distant mountain range and providing an intimate seating area around a massive stone fireplace. Like campgoers of the past, families and friends warm themselves around the fire on chilly nights. On sunny days, they relax in the long row of rocking chairs on the front porch. Everything is as it would have been in the camps of the late nineteenth century that inspired us.

The porch that wraps around three sides of the dining hall includes an outdoor dining area where campgoers enjoy meals amidst mountain breezes and spectacular views. Columns made of young locust trees with the bark remaining and decorative brackets culled from branches reflect the porch's treetop setting.

SENSE OF TIME

*Familiarity lies at the heart
of comfort—and familiarity
comes only with the passage
of time and the appreciation
of its gifts.*

IN OLD HOUSES, antique beams conjure images of the hands that planed them, and floorboards bear traces of those who walked upon them years before. There is something about having had generations of inhabitants that gives a house soul and provides those who live in it a deep sense of comfort and belonging. Most of our clients desire houses with this spirit of age, but they also want modern amenities. We have learned to resolve this dichotomy through an approach we call "generational architecture."

Rooted in the study of tradition, this methodology allows us to see with the eyes of the past to design houses for the present. The process often includes the invention of narratives that guide our designs—imaginary backstories that are based on historical precedent. First, we establish what the "original" structure might have looked like and how it was used. Then we consider how it might have been altered over time to meet the changing needs of successive generations. Translating these narratives into reality, we weave form, materials, and craftsmanship together to create new environments that are rich with the texture and nuance of age.

One way to create the impression of time's passage is "unbundling" houses with wings, breezeways, and outbuildings that appear to have been added over time. The common practice of enclosing porches to increase interior space is another precedent we draw from. "Mama got electricity" is a saying we use to explain why porches were often transformed into kitchens when electricity and modern appliances became available. In this spirit, we add layers of history to houses by including kitchens, dining rooms, and other spaces that resemble old porches enclosed by previous generations.

The repurposing of agrarian buildings for residential use—a frequent occurrence when farms declined—suggests another approach to "generational architecture." Sometimes we literally repurpose old buildings, salvaging antique structures like the pair of chinked log houses we reassembled into a guesthouse. In other cases, we build history from the ground up, designing new structures that appear to be antique ones that have been remodeled for new purposes—a house in the shape of an old dairy barn or a hunting lodge resembling a cotton warehouse.

One of the most concrete, yet also subliminal, ways to borrow time is through the use of antique and traditional materials. A house constructed with hand-planed boards or beams from old barns surrounds those who live in it with the fabric of the past. If they are historically accurate or indigenous, new materials can create just as palpable a sense of history. Freshly made tabby foundations, hand-molded brick stairs, standing-seam metal roofs, and cedar plank walls forge a tangible link between the past and the present.

Even if built with the best materials, a house will not feel right unless constructed with great precision and skill. In the work of the great architects and carpenters of the past, every detail was an act of love. When we create houses, we rely upon master builders and craftsmen who practice the old ways of working. They know how to use hand tools and understand traditional carpentry such as true post-and-beam construction and mortise-and-tenon joinery. Together, we are part of a lineage that creates houses that will be lived in and loved by generations.

PAGE 157: *Finished with a distressed paint surface, handsome woodwork recalling the grandeur of the Georgian era gives this living room the authentic appearance of an eighteenth-century dwelling, despite its having been built in the late twentieth century.* ABOVE: *The weathered surface of pine shutters and the rusted tin of an old kerosene lantern endow this cottage with the patina of age.*

Borrowing Time

RIDGELAND, SOUTH CAROLINA

All the elements of a small nineteenth-century plantation can be found on this rural property—a gracious house with a wraparound porch, a cotton warehouse, and bunkhouses for farm workers. But when we first set foot on the land, there was just one lone live oak and 1,000 acres of slash pine. When our client asked us to design a hunting plantation on this empty piece of land, he wanted it to look and feel as though it had been there for more than a century. Informed by his knowledge of history, he envisioned a compound resembling a modest post–Civil War plantation that had been transformed into a hunting retreat in the early twentieth century—a common occurrence in the wake of tenant farming.

By the time we became involved, the client had already discovered an old farmhouse that he wanted to move to the property and turn into its plantation house. Built in 1914, this abandoned building was in desperate need of repair, but it had the old-fashioned simplicity and center-hall floor plan he desired. The moment he showed it to us, we realized that we could literally borrow time by moving the old house to a knoll overlooking a lake, where it would become the new plantation's centerpiece.

The first thing we considered was what this house would have looked like had it always stood on the property. Our answer is that it would have been a typical raised Lowcountry house with deep porches to cool and shade the rooms within. Because the old house's original front and back porches were dilapidated beyond repair, we replaced them with new ones that surround the house on four sides. Adding stature and an air of genteel dignity, they also provided the room we needed to enlarge the house without interfering with its original shape and structure.

Leaving the front porch open, we modified the back portions to suggest that they had been enclosed in the early twentieth century to accommodate additional rooms, including a

RIGHT: *The house's central stair hall terminates in a newly constructed door that mimics the shape, size, and trim of the front door at the other end of the hall. Designed to create the impression that it was once the back door, it opens to a sunny sitting room that was added to the rear of the house.* OVERLEAF: *The raised foundation, metal roof, and dormers are details typical of raised cottages throughout the South.*

kitchen, sunroom, and master bath. To create the illusion that these new spaces were once part of an original porch, we designed walls of windows that fit between floor-to-ceiling posts matching those on the front of the house.

To be consistent with vernacular architecture, we avoided overly refined and embellished material throughout the renovation. Much of the beadboard on the walls and ceiling was salvaged from the original house. When additional beadboard was required, the newly purchased material matched the original perfectly, even though a century had passed. Local craftsmen built doors, windows, and cabinetry faithful to the period and style of the original

home. Although the original staircase had deteriorated beyond the point of repair, it was reproduced exactly to maintain the historical authenticity and integrity of the home.

Across the lake, the tin roofs of what seem to be a cotton warehouse, cane mill, and bunkhouses shine in the sun. Seen from the house, these appear to be entirely utilitarian. On closer inspection, however, it becomes evident that they include a rustic but comfortable hunting lodge and several guest cabins, seemingly repurposed in the early twentieth century from their agricultural origins.

Unlike the main house, where salvaged materials had the authentic patina of age, the new lodge needed to acquire instant history. To create the illusion of time's passage, we designed a single-gable structure typical of nineteenth-century farm warehouses. A series of shed-roof porches attached to the building appear to have been added on piecemeal fashion in the early twentieth century.

LEFT: *On the front porch, a light blue tongue-and-groove ceiling, old-fashioned ceiling fans, and hanging lanterns create a tranquil setting from which to sit in rocking chairs and survey the landscape.* ABOVE: *The low hipped roof that surrounds the house shelters both the open porch on the front and enclosed additions on the rear. This arrangement prevents the addition of new rooms from overwhelming the proportions of the original house.*

On the exterior, plain, easily available materials common to agrarian buildings were used, including tin roofing and pine exterior siding. Inside the structure, the vaulted ceiling and exposed trusses are also true to nineteenth-century construction methods, but the brick fireplace and more modern walls of windows provide "evidence" of the building's fictional repurposing as a hunting lodge.

In the bunkhouses, tin roofs, board-and-batten siding, and plain pine-plank walls demonstrate the same traditional approach. The humble buildings that might once have provided basic shelter for farm workers now accommodate visiting hunters. Not much larger than three hundred square feet, they provide just enough space for two people to sleep and hang their clothes. The only thing that might have been changed during their imaginary repurposing is the addition of plumbing and air-conditioning.

ABOVE: *One of four original rooms flanking the house's center hall, the dining room has the simple trim and walls of old beadboard that are common to Southern farmhouses. A primitive corner cupboard adds another authentic element of history to the room.* RIGHT: *Four small bedrooms were added to the spaces beneath the roof's gables. Their new beadboard walls and trim create a vintage look that complements the rooms below.*

It takes imagination to make a project like this successful. But good fortune also played an important role. We were lucky to find the old house that rooted the compound so deeply in the region's past. And the house was lucky to find us. By salvaging it, we reclaimed time and were able to make history where little had existed before.

ABOVE: *In the master bathroom, windows fitted between pilasters that resemble porch posts create the illusion that this room was claimed from an old back porch. The freestanding vanity and claw-foot tub are like those that would have been found in a bathroom added on to a house in the 1930s.* RIGHT: *A painted worktable, a farmhouse sink, wooden counters, and simple cabinets add vintage charm to a kitchen that also appears to have once been a porch.*

Creating the appearance of an old waterside warehouse modified more than once in its history, an attached pair of shed roofs slopes gradually down from the gable of the building that serves as a hunting and fishing lodge. Beneath them, a porch that appears to have been added to the fictional warehouse cantilevers over the lake, providing guests with a cool place to relax and enjoy the view.

ABOVE: *Seen from across the lake at sunset, this picturesque hunting lodge casts a warm glow.* TOP RIGHT: *On the façades of matching bunkhouses, porches covered by tin shed roofs provide the perfect place to sit and watch the shimmering reflections on the lake.* BOTTOM RIGHT: *With tall windows and a door that opens to a corner porch, the lodge's dining room appears to hover over the lake. Painted wood floors and well-worn furnishings create a comfortable atmosphere appropriate to a hunting lodge.*

Barn Raising

SPRING ISLAND, SOUTH CAROLINA

We have deep appreciation for buildings that have been repurposed at some point during their history. This practice was common in the past, when people were less ready to tear down old buildings and more interested in salvaging them. Designing new residences that appear to be repurposed utilitarian or agrarian structures endows them with a rich sense of history. On Spring Island, where rural farm-style buildings blend easily among the open fields, dirt roads, old oaks, and pine forests, the idea is particularly appropriate.

When we began this project, our clients showed us an article about an old dairy barn transformed into a residence. Attached was a note that said "FUN—Don't want to live in a barn but love some adaptations." A family of four, our clients lived in a Greek Revival house in New Jersey and were drawn to the idea of a relaxed, informal environment for their second home. Beginning with the concept of a converted barn and expanding it with a bit of whimsy, we designed an entire compound with an imaginary past, including a farm manager's office turned into a master bedroom wing, a tractor-shed garage, and a guesthouse shaped like a chicken coop. When you come around the drive and see it for the first time, the experience is like discovering an old farm tucked away in the countryside.

In projects like these, we often reach far into the past to salvage rustic materials and sometimes even entire buildings from primitive subsistence farms. In this case, we looked back little more than a century. Envisioning the "original" building as a circa-1900 commercial dairy barn, we purchased new machine-milled lumber, plank siding, and metal roof and flues like those used at that time. Although the materials are postindustrial, the shape of the barn, with its sloping tin roof, sliding barn doors, and cupola topped with a weathercock, is timeless and iconic.

Massive barn doors serve as an unconventional entrance, sliding open to a large breezeway that separates the two sides of the house. Wide enough for a wagon to stand in while

At the main entry, sliding barn doors open to a central space that bisects the barn-style house and divides the children's living area from the family rooms and master bedroom wing.

Less rustic than the dark, unpainted wood barns of the late eighteenth and early nineteenth centuries, the building is painted in light shades of ochre and green that complement the surrounding landscape. Prop shutters that protect the interior from direct sun can be closed for protection from storms.

ABOVE: *Dormer windows illuminate a bunkroom for children, which connects to a reading loft on the other side of the barn via a metal bridge.* RIGHT: *Fitted with large sliding screen doors on either end, the passageway in the house's center is a sheltered spot where the family can sit and enjoy the breeze or warm themselves by the brick fireplace.*

A wall of simple cupboards separates the porch-like dining room from the kitchen. Juxtaposed against the living area's wood floor, the concrete slab of the dining room reinforces the impression that this was once an open-air space that was subsequently enclosed.

receiving bales of hay from the hayloft above, this would also have served as a threshing floor in the building's fictional past. Illuminated by the cupola and warmed with a brick fireplace, it now functions as an open-air passageway dividing the children's living area from the communal spaces on the other side. Pocket screens on the front and French doors opening to a screened porch on the back give the space an additional purpose as an indoor-outdoor living area.

In the children's realm, a secret ladder-style stair and sleeping bunks squeezed beneath the hayloft roof suggest that every nook and cranny was used when the barn was turned into a home. A metal bridge stretches from the hayloft across the breezeway to a small room overlooking the kitchen, from which the children can communicate with their parents.

The open-plan kitchen and family room fills most of the space on the other side of the barn. Pine-plank walls, rough-hewn beams, and heavy trusses give the area a rugged agrarian appearance. To avoid any intrusion of the modern age, we disguised the kitchen appliances. Both a range hood resembling something fashioned from old farming materials and a refrigerator fitted with tin pie-safe-style panels reinforce the room's rural aesthetic.

What seems once to have been a porch with rough timber posts and a shed roof now accommodates a dining room and screened-in living area. In the dining room, tall casement windows typical of those used in the first half of the twentieth century fill the gaps between the porch-style posts. On one end of the room, French doors lead to the screened porch, and on the other end, a red barn door slides open to reveal a cozy family room.

A small wing extending toward the back of the property includes a master suite and home office. Joined to the barn by a small breezeway, it appears to have once been a separate building—perhaps the farm manager's office—later attached to the building to provide more living space. With windows framing views of the Lowcountry landscape and a small porch with just enough space for two rocking chairs, the quiet wing provides the adults their own domain.

Throughout the design process, we applied the same sense of economy and ingenuity that those before us had brought to the practice of repurposing. With history—both real and imaginary—as our guide, we created a house, which though new, has the warmth and welcoming atmosphere of a building that has been used and reused for more than a century.

LEFT: *In the combined kitchen and living room, heavy weathered beams recall the structure of a timber-frame barn. A window high in the wall overlooking the living area opens into a hayloft-like space that serves as the children's reading room.* OVERLEAF: *On the rear of the house, casement windows enclose the dining room and walls of screens shelter a screened porch where friends and family enjoy relaxing together.*

Island Homestead

SPRING ISLAND, SOUTH CAROLINA

Three houses stand beneath the pines and oaks that shade this marsh-front piece of land: a nineteenth-century-style cottage with tall gables and pilasters around its wide front door, a modest white-clapboard guesthouse in the style of an old farmhouse, and a log house with rough-hewn beams and dovetail joints. This rustic building appears to be the oldest structure on the property but in reality, it's the most recent addition—a second guesthouse commissioned by our clients to accommodate their growing family and visiting friends.

When we design a compound, the buildings rarely appear to have been built at the same time. Often inspired by fictional narratives, the structures work together to tell a story about past generations who lived in them over a period of many years. The guiding narrative for this compound was inspired by pioneer farmsteads where settlers built log houses using raw natural materials and rudimentary building techniques. As new generations were born and remained to work on the farms, additional dwellings were often built. Constructed with increasingly sophisticated carpentry and building materials, these reflected shifting styles and the growing affluence of their owners.

Imagining that the two buildings already standing on this property were latter-day additions to a prospering farm, we decided that the third should appear to be the original homesteaders' house. With the help of a dealer specializing in salvaged materials, we located two one-room log houses that were transported to the site and reassembled. Placing them side by side, we joined them beneath a single roof to create a form known as a dogtrot. Named for the central open-air passageways through which a dog could trot, this type of house was common in the agrarian South. Over time, residents often enclosed the open-air passages to form center halls like the one we created to divide the master bedroom from a large living room on the other side of the house.

In the guesthouse bedroom, walls of square-hewn logs with plaster chinking provide a cool, restful retreat from the Lowcountry sun. Simple furnishings, including an antique brass bed and quilt, are perfect complements to the rustic architecture.

Surrounded by mature trees and dense undergrowth, the house appears to have stood on this site for centuries. When the two original log houses were combined, a pitched tin roof was added to create space for sleeping lofts and provide a deep over-hang to shelter the porch.

LEFT: *Although the porch is all new construction, its ceiling and posts of reclaimed barn wood create an antique appearance.* ABOVE: *Working in traditional methods, craftsmen reassembled the numbered pieces of the old structures, fitting together original dovetail joints and chinking the spaces between the hewn logs with plaster.*

Throughout the building process, we maintained the original character of the salvaged structures while taking liberties to create more livable spaces. A shed-roof addition at one end of the hall accommodates a small but modern kitchen. A sixteen-foot-deep porch that wraps around the house replaces the narrow, more utilitarian porch typically associated with log houses. Adding tall gables, we raised the low ceilings inside the rooms and created space for sleeping lofts. In the manner of early settlers who frequently recycled building materials when they lacked access to new ones, we clad the gables with reclaimed barn wood still tinged with red paint.

Together, the form and materials of the guesthouse forge a direct connection with history. Rooted in tradition, the log house offers a respite from the hectic pace of modern life. Sitting on its porch, you can listen to the pine trees rustle and creak just as the pioneers did. Stepping inside, you enter into a wood-scented place where the past is tangibly present.

Primitive ladders lead to a pair of lofts overlooking the living room. Converted gas lanterns, checked valances, and country antiques, combined with the room's log walls and antique heart-pine floors, establish a rustic atmosphere.

193

ABOVE: *Like many kitchens added to nineteenth-century houses when modern plumbing and electricity became available, the small, utilitarian room extends from the rear of the house as a shed-style structure.* RIGHT: *In the tradition of rural homesteaders who often built with salvaged materials, the ceiling of the living room is covered with reclaimed boards of random width and patina.*

Generational Cottage

SPRING ISLAND, SOUTH CAROLINA

S itting by the side of a winding, unpaved road, this simple cottage greets passersby with a friendly, modest air. Its painted metal roof, shiplap walls, and board-and-batten shutters speak of a family concerned more with shelter than show. Calling to mind the humble houses of the rural South, it appears to be a small one-bedroom dwelling—an impression that is deceiving. Behind the little house, three more buildings spread across the site.

When clients asked us to design this retreat, they requested something intimate enough for a couple to enjoy a quiet getaway yet spacious enough for larger groups to share time together without sacrificing privacy. Because it was to be one of the first houses on Spring Island, it was also important that the house establish the unpretentious scale and appearance appropriate to the quiet, close-to-nature community.

Turning to the past for inspiration, we imagined a historical narrative in which the home of a small family grew over time to include separate dwellings for subsequent generations. Drawing from this common precedent, we "unbundled" the mass of the house into a primary dwelling with three cottages linked by porches and breezeways. Each with its own entrance and private screened porch, the cottages have varying rooflines and window styles that suggest a country carpenter built them one at a time.

Well-crafted simplicity combined with the quirks and unsophisticated functionalism of rural architecture creates an atmosphere of old-fashioned charm. Beadboard wainscoting and planks of wood cover the walls, ceilings, and floors. In the kitchen, cabinets fitted with chicken-wire doors suggest the ingenuity of a carpenter working with readily available materials. Rudimentary closets in the master and guest bedrooms, in which cotton curtains take the place of doors, tell the same tale.

A converted kerosene lantern and shutters with weathered green paint and primitive shutter dogs suggest that this cottage was built more than a century ago.

Exposed rafter tails, plain porch posts, and simple railings contribute to the unpretentious charm of this Lowcountry dwelling. Wings resembling additions to a small country cottage extend from one end of the house to accommodate the master bedroom and bath.

Every detail, from the painted wood floors and handmade quilts of the bedrooms to the exposed-brick fireplace and flea-market finds in the living room, was carefully chosen to evoke the honest simplicity of days gone by. Rather than installing modern or reproduction lighting, we chose vintage oil lamps from a gallery specializing in salvaged and retrofitted light fixtures, setting them on shelf brackets throughout the house. Reminiscent of the days when lanterns like these were carried from room to room at night, they recall memories of life before electricity.

Although thoughtful choices of materials and decorative details gave the compound a sense of history, a fortuitous mistake added even more depth and character. To enhance the main house's cozy atmosphere, we decided to paint the living room and kitchen ceilings a deep shade of red. When the paint dried, however, it looked too shiny and new. After the workers sanded it down in preparation for applying a lighter shade, subtle vestiges of red paint remained, creating a time-weathered quality we never could have anticipated.

LEFT: *Washed with light blue-green paint, the pine-plank walls of the living room have a patina that suggests the passage of time.* ABOVE: *Floating cabinets with chicken-wire doors create a transparent divider between the kitchen and living room. Contrasting with the kitchen's heart-pine countertops, stainless steel appliances suggest a modern renovation, adding another layer of history to the house.*

Although there was nothing unplanned about the arrangement of cottages behind the house, their haphazard placement suggests otherwise. Rambling down a gentle slope toward a tidal pond, they loosely embrace a courtyard ideal for outdoor entertainments on cool days. When the weather heats up, a spacious porch behind the main house overlooking the courtyard is the place to be. With wicker furniture arranged beneath old-fashioned ceiling fans, it is a comfortable outdoor living room where family and friends come together to rest and enjoy each other's company.

ABOVE: *In one of the guest cottages, rag rugs and a pair of brass twin beds recall memories of old-fashioned bedrooms in small-town Southern houses.* RIGHT: *In another guest cottage, the bathroom's beadboard wainscoting, blinds with wooden slats, a claw-foot tub, and porcelain doorknobs are also souvenirs of bygone days.*

When we talk about this house, we like to say, "It's so bad, it's good." The seemingly piecemeal progression of buildings, the faded red ceiling, the primitive camp lanterns, and the creaky screen doors that slam when they shut are the very things that make it feel genuine and welcoming. This is not a house pretending to be anything other than what it is—a country place where family and friends come together to enjoy life across the generations.

LEFT: *Deep and wide, the back porch is a comfortable outdoor living space where family and friends while away the hours beneath whirring ceiling fans. The primary communal gathering space, it opens to the living and dining rooms through several French doors.* ABOVE: *Each cottage has a private porch, including this screened porch, which overlooks a backyard filled with azaleas and native plants.*

Reclaiming Time

SPRING ISLAND, SOUTH CAROLINA

Reclaimed materials that bear evidence of traditional craftsmanship and vestiges of use are touchstones that connect us with the past. When a client asked us to design a guesthouse resembling an old barn, we borrowed not only the form of nineteenth-century barns but also their materials to create a building that looks as though it had stood beneath the oaks for a century or more. Every detail, from the weathered siding to the antique hay hook hanging from its gable, convinces those who pass that it is part of Spring Island's original architecture.

The client grew up on a farm in North Carolina but left that life behind to become a doctor. However, his longtime dream was to have a place that would be a bridge back to the past, reconnecting him and his family to his rural roots. With the help of a Tennessee dealer of salvaged materials, we found exactly the ingredients we needed in the form of boards, beams, and even an entire staircase from abandoned farm buildings.

Set back from a country road, the barn stands on a grassy plot of land along the Colleton River, an estuary that flows with the tides between wide marshy banks. Constructed with irregular planks and beams of oak aged to a silvery patina, the building blends right into the landscape of Spanish moss–covered oaks. Timeworn wood covers every surface except the tin roof, including walls, doors, window sashes, and shutters. Reminiscent of agrarian ingenuity, even the twelve-foot-high hayloft shutters operated by a rope-and-pulley system appear authentic.

More in keeping with traditional agrarian style, heavy barn doors slide open to reveal a large open space where livestock and farm equipment would have been kept. Now it is a place where family and friends gather around the table to enjoy Lowcountry dinners of fresh-caught shrimp and local corn. Constructed almost entirely of reclaimed wood, with plank walls and a ceiling of rough, exposed rafters, the area recalls the undisguised functionalism of

The barn-style guesthouse is constructed of salvaged barn wood, some of it more than two hundred years old. Many of the old oak boards were so hard that pilot holes had to be drilled before nails could be driven into them. An iconic cupola with a weathercock crowns the building's V-crimp metal roof, bringing light into the interior spaces.

Built entirely of salvaged wood, the new barn is almost impossible to distinguish from the farm buildings that inspired it. Sliding doors, a hayloft-style window, and an antique hay hook complete its resemblance to a working barn. On either side of the hayloft window, twelve-foot-tall shutters operated by a pulley system can be drawn up beneath the gables in case of storms.

working barns. In the apparent repurposing of the space, we did little to change its primitive appearance, only adding a bathroom and building a partition wall to screen an office and bunk bedroom.

The front of the house faces the river and an oak-studded lawn that slopes down slightly to a deepwater dock. We couldn't resist adding a two-story porch overlooking this view, although a real barn would not have had one. Using traditional timber-frame construction and salvaged beams like those found elsewhere in the barn, we resolved the inconsistency to create a porch that complemented the agrarian building.

Passing through a heavy plank door beneath the porch, you stand at the foot of a stair-case that shows signs of wear and tear. Unlike many of the materials we used in the project, which were cut and assembled to fit the design, the pieces of this staircase were carefully

ABOVE: *A timber-frame porch faces the wide river at the property's edge. Rough cedar logs sawn in half lengthwise form the floor and ceiling between the porch's lower and upper levels.* RIGHT: *In keeping with the building's primitive style, the porch floor is laid with old Savannah gray brick assembled without mortar. The rust-red door opens to a stairwell that leads to the second-floor living area.*

reassembled in their original position. Worn by long use, the treads dip slightly in the middle and the newel post's smooth surface shows the touch of many hands. This evidence of long use, combined with the scent of antique pine, evokes an immediate sense of nostalgia the moment you enter.

At the top of the stairs, a family room just large enough for a pair of overstuffed leather chairs, a writing desk, a small dinner table, and an alcove kitchen fills the space beneath the roof's gable. Antique boards turning silver with age cover every surface, from the walls and ceilings to the bedroom doors and kitchen cabinets. Deep notches cut into hand-hewn beams

that span the ceiling show where they once were joined, mortise-and-tenon style, in the barns from which they came. While it might go unnoticed, this detail is just one of many that trigger collective memories. The soft gray silhouette of the barn beneath the oaks, the texture and scent of the wood, and the sound of creaking boards all work together to connect the client and his family to the past.

LEFT: *The second floor of the barn consists of one main room that combines a living and dining area with an alcove kitchen beneath a hayloft bunkroom.* ABOVE: *Barn-style sliding doors create privacy for the bedrooms opening off the main room. Fashioned from the same weathered oak boards that cover the walls and floors, platform beds include drawers for storage.*

THE DESIGN PROCESS

Whether designing a country house, large family estate, vacation cottage, or town house, Historical Concepts begins each project by studying the site and the vernacular architecture of the area. The process then finds expression in freehand sketches that explore form and style, merging the client's desires with regional traditions. Representing a response that is both traditional and creative, these schematic designs echo the pride and artistry that architects of the past brought to their work.

As the process unfolds, these freehand sketches are interpreted into precise, computer-generated designs that weave the proportions and building methods of the past with newly conceived floor plans and elevations. Original ideas take shape in detailed representations that are both rooted in history and appropriate to modern ways of living.

The final stage is the creation of construction documents that convey meticulous measurements and specifications, including appropriate materials and finishes. These plans ensure that the end result will reflect the attention to detail and respect for craftsmanship that traditionally trained architects and tradesmen brought to their work. The depth and breadth of this documentation is necessary to ensure that builders and craftsmen perform at their best, and in so doing, revive a tradition of handcrafted excellence.

This hand-drawn study of the front door of a quintessential Lowcountry house expresses careful attention to scale, proportion, and detail. In the drawing, compositional elements including sidelight panels, engaged columns, and pilasters and their capitals have been refined to complement their man-made setting and natural surroundings. Throughout the process, every aspect of the final design evolves into a house with a sense of timeless history.

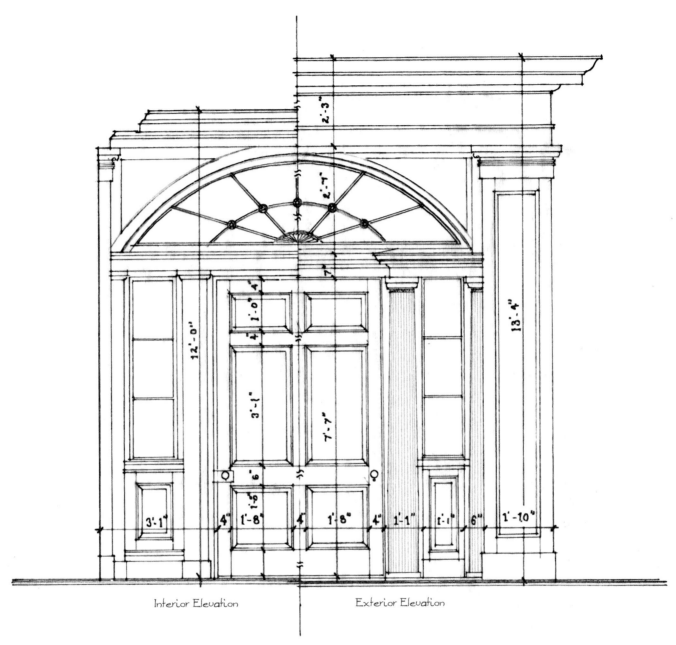

Interior Elevation   Exterior Elevation

FRONT DOOR STUDY
COMPOSITE SKETCH

RESOURCES

It takes many talented individuals to create a well-crafted home, and the South is rich with design resources. The artistry of many of the best interior designers, craftsmen, builders, and landscape architects is featured in *Coming Home.*

The legacies of the late Robert Marvin, considered by many as the landscape architect emeritus of the Lowcountry (pages 37–47, cover), and custom homebuilder Howard L. Griffin Sr. (pages 4–5, 170–73) are also honored herein.

INTERIOR DESIGNERS
With a penchant for traditional design, these featured designers have created stylishly comfortable interiors.

The Ballance Group, Inc. (Anne Parker Ballance)
Beaufort, South Carolina / 843.524.2287
ballancegroup.com
pages 35, 187–95

Susan B. Bozeman Designs, Inc. (Susan Bozeman)
Atlanta, Georgia / 404.237.7745
pages 83–91

Davis Design (Melanie Davis)
Atlanta, Georgia / 678.362.3951
melaniedavis.com
pages 18, 135–45

Ruth Edwards Antiques and Interiors
(Ruth Edwards)
Hilton Head, South Carolina / 843.671.2223
pages 37–59, 161–73, 197–205

S. R. Gambrel, Inc. (Steven Gambrel)
New York, New York / 212.925.3380
srgambrel.com
pages 71–81

Paula Grulee Designs (Paula Grulee)
Cincinnati, Ohio / 513.871.6718
pages 207–13

Carolyn Hultman Interior Design
(Carolyn Hultman)
Savannah, Georgia / 912.236.0111
carolynhultman.com
pages 61–69

Inside (Suzanne Watson)
Grayton Beach, Florida / 850.685.5504
inside–inc.com
pages 22–23

J Banks Design
(Joni Vanderslice and Shelley Wilkins)
Hilton Head, South Carolina / 843.681.5122
jbanksdesign.com
pages 119–33

Miriam Jordan Interiors (Miriam Jordan Ricks)
Charleston, South Carolina / 843.884.2840
pages 105–17

3D by D Designs (Diane Makgill)
Raleigh, North Carolina / 919.413.0181
3dbyddesigns.com
pages 175–85

Barbara N. Yergens Interiors, Inc.
(Barbara Yergens)
Beaufort, South Carolina
pages 147–55

ARCHITECTURAL AND
DECORATIVE ELEMENTS
*With an appreciation for the past, these artisans
and antiques dealers offer furnishings and
finishes to complement the classic home.*

AAA World Floors (Bill Riley)
Clarkston, Georgia / 404.373.3993
(antique lumber and flooring)

Architectural Accents (Maria A. Williamson)
Atlanta, Georgia / 404.266.8700
architecturalaccents.com
(architectural antiques)

Joe Doolan
Hilton Head, South Carolina
843.341.3233
josephdoolan.com
(murals and Old World finishes)

Fracasso Woodworking and Cabinetry
Walterboro, South Carolina / 843.538.3822
(cabinetmaker)

McDaniel Cook Cabinetmakers
Athens, Georgia / 706.338.3634
mcdanielcook.googlepages.com
(custom furniture and woodwork)

Eloise Pickard
Adairsville, Georgia / 404.252.3244
(antique lighting)

Randall Brothers, Inc.
Atlanta, Georgia / 404.892.6666
randallbrothers.com
(millwork and moldings)

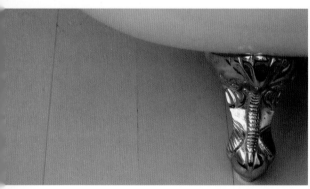

Southern Stair Builders (Don Ouimette)
Hilton Head, South Carolina / 843.422.2887
(custom stair builder)

Stewart Brannen Millwork Company
Register, Georgia / 912.488.2397
brannenmillwork.com
(millwork and moldings)

Vintage Lumber Sales, Inc. (Willis Everett)
Gay, Georgia / 706.538.0180
vintagelumbersales.com
(antique lumber and flooring)

BUILDERS
*With attention to detail and fine craftsmanship,
these custom builders have translated
architectural drawings into timeless buildings.*

Cambridge Homes, Inc.
Hilton Head, South Carolina
843.341.2444
cambridgebuilding.com
pages 15, 37–47, 99 (far right), cover

Chechessee Construction Company
Okatie, South Carolina / 843.812.9512
pages 35, 187–95

Clark and Leatherwood, Inc.
Waynesville, North Carolina / 828.452.4500
clarkandleatherwood.com
pages 147–54

Clements Construction of Frogmore
Beaufort, South Carolina / 843.521.7171
pages 11 (top left and center)17, 19, 119–33,
207–13, 222

Fraser Construction, Inc.
Bluffton, South Carolina / 843.815.4747
fraser–construction.net
pages 98 (center), 101 (top left)

Genesis Construction
Bluffton, South Carolina / 843.757.8220
genesis–construction.com
pages 49–59, 97, 101 (top right, bottom left and right), 103

L. M. Jones Construction
Beaufort, South Carolina / 843.592.1103
pages 1, 9, 12, 83–91, 175–85, 197–205

MJR Builders
Bluffton, South Carolina / 843.706.2288
(with Lawrence Construction / Hilton Head, South Carolina)
pages 33, 93, 157

Pinckney Brothers, Inc.
Hilton Head, South Carolina
843.681.8153
pages 61–69

Pine Mountain Builders
Pine Mountain, Georgia / 770.859.9100
page 95

Sands Construction Company, Inc.
Hobe Sound, Florida / 772.546.2111
pages 2, 11 (middle left, bottom left)

Shelco, Inc.
Charlotte, North Carolina / 704.367.5600
shelcoinc.com
page 98 (left)

David Steele
Charleston, South Carolina
eastcoastwip.com
pages 16, 105–17

Watermark Homes of North Carolina
Oriental, North Carolina / 252.249.3371
watermarkhomesnc.net
page 11 (top right, center right)

Willis Sinclair Homes
Lodge, South Carolina / 843.846.2500
willissinclair.com
pages 161–69

Windward Builders
Sag Harbor, New York / 631.899.3489
windwardbuildersny.com
pages 11 (bottom right), 71–81

The Woodruff Companies (Bruce Jones)
Columbus, Georgia / 706.323.6401
woodruffre.com
pages 135–45

LANDSCAPE ARCHITECTS
AND DESIGNERS
To create a sense of place, these landscape architects and designers seamlessly unite the man-made with the natural surroundings.

HighGrove Partners
(William C. Lincicome and Erik Jarkins)
Austell, Georgia / 678.298.0550
highgrove.net
pages 135–45

Donald Hooten
Decatur, Georgia / 404.373.9816
pages 1, 4, 12, 61–69, 83–91, 105–33, 161–205

Innocenti and Webel (Linda R. Zylman)
Hobe Sound, Florida / 772.546.9650
pages 2, 11 (bottom left)

P. Allen Smith and Associates
Little Rock, Arkansas / 501.376.1894
pallensmithandassociates.com
pages 71–81

ACKNOWLEDGMENTS

Coming Home is the product of a decades-long journey inscribed by the people, places, and experiences I have encountered along the way. I have been humbled by the generosity and encouragement of countless individuals, and I am honored to name just a few of them here.

To the educators who shared their passions and, in doing so, helped me discover mine: Thank you to Austin Lowery and Ronald Arnholm of the University of Georgia for exposing me to the principles of design and encouraging me to continue my education. I am indebted to Alvin Eisenmann for giving me the opportunity to attend Yale as a student in the graduate graphic design program. I will always remember Charles Moore, Dean of the Yale School of Architecture, for his sense of humor and playfulness that he brought into his work and his teachings, and his successor, Herman Spiegel, for opening the School of Architecture to me and for his positive outlook on life and learning.

To the developers who gave us an opportunity to succeed: Thank you to Vince Graham, Bob Turner, Peter Rummell, Joe Barnes, and the late Scott Hudgens for taking a chance on traditional architecture and urbanism in those early days. I would like to express my gratitude to Jim and Betsy Chaffin for having the clear vision that has gifted us with Spring Island, an extraordinary place, and to Jim Anthony for giving us the chance to work on such an idyllic canvas. I also thank the developers of Oldfield, Palmetto Bluff, The Ford Plantation, Balsam Mountain Preserve, WaterColor, and River Dunes, for allowing us to leave a mark on the communities you have created. Finally, I am indebted to Bill Loflin, our supporter, promoter, and friend at Spring Island.

To those who have practiced by my side now and in the past: Thank you for the beautiful work that fills these pages. *Coming Home* owes its existence to my partners, Terry Pylant, Todd Strickland, Aaron Daily, Andrew Cogar, and Kevin Clark. You lift me up every day and inspire me with your understanding of the past and your eye for the present. To the talented team that I am so proud of—David Bryant, Christopher Carrigan, J. P. Curran, Elizabeth Dillon, Chris Eiland, Sandra Guritz, Paul Knight, Lindsay LaBudde, Nina Meyer, Colleen O'Keeffe, Dan Osborne, Becca Pendley, Jessi Pierce, Clay Rokicki, Forest Sickles, Domenick Treschitta, David VanGroningen, and Claire Watson—your enthusiasm, creativity, and work ethic are second to none. My thanks, also, to those former associates who contributed to many of the projects featured in this book, including my daughter, Suzanne Stern, and

Sharon Bray, Zhi Feng, Nate Hickey, Bhoke Manga, Marty Mullin, Megan Nelson, Joshua Roland, Samantha Salden, Deepna Sarkar, Jeremy Sommer, and Ryan and Shaun Yurcaba. I am so grateful to have had the late Philip Windsor, a gifted architect, by my side for the early part of this journey, and equally thankful to have Dan Lemberg, consulting architect, and Donald Hooten, landscape architect, still with me after all these years. To Eloise Pickard, whose lighting is a work of art, and Willis Everett, whose reclaimed lumber has added the patina of the past to our homes: Thank you for your craft and for the warmth of your friendship.

To those that work behind the scenes: Todd Strickland, my partner and son—thank you for taking on the business of doing business, which leaves me free to do what I do best. My appreciation also goes to my administrative team—Dawn Fritz, Anne Marie Noll, Laurie Pennywitt, Laura Strickland, Linda Strickland, and Kristy Tindall—who are all-stars in their own right.

To those that work with their hands, building the homes we design: Thank you for carrying on the building arts. You are the unsung heroes of this book and your craftsmanship is a legacy to future generations.

To those who took interest in our work and shared it with a broader audience: We owe much to the many publications that have featured our projects. Special thanks to *Southern Progress*, the first to "take us to the dance," for giving us a place in your pages through the years and the opportunity to design many of your Idea Houses.

To those who are directly responsible for *Coming Home*: My gratitude to Charles Miers, Rizzoli's publisher, for deeming our work worthy of a book. To Sandy Gilbert Freidus, the most patient of editors: Thank you for those times you stuck to your guns. This book is better for it. My hat goes off to the editorial team, Maria Pia Gramaglia, Hilary Ney, Jessica O'Neil, and Elizabeth Smith; and the many talented photographers who captured our work on film. Thank you also to Eric Mueller of Element Group for a book design that is quiet and elegant, befitting the homes within. My sincere appreciation goes to Susan Sully, a most talented writer and Southern cosmopolitan, for making sense of my thoughts and so eloquently articulating them in written form. Finally, a very special thank you goes to Dawn Fritz, Historical Concepts' multitalented marketing manager, whose even-keeled personality always managed to keep the herd heading west.

Without a doubt, my deepest and everlasting gratitude goes to our clients. Thank you for entrusting me with your dreams, and for giving me the opportunity to live mine.

OVERLEAF: *The rear façade of a Greek Revival–style house in a dramatic Lowcountry setting is the result of extraordinary attention to detail. With walls of windows that recede between Classical symmetrical wings, it both reflects and reveals the scenery that surrounds it.*